Love, Julie

# UNDER THE RUG

## Black Lace and Barbie Doll Heads

Julie Gillen

PUBLISHED BY WESTVIEW, INC.
KINGSTON SPRINGS, TENNESSEE

PUBLISHED BY WESTVIEW, INC.
P.O. Box 605
Kingston Springs, TN 37082
www.publishedbywestview.com

© 2013 Julie Gillen
All rights reserved, including the right to reproduction in whole or in part in any form.

ISBN 978-1-937763-94-7

First edition, May 2013

Cover photo by Tim Yeager

These articles were originally printed in *The Daily Herald.*

Good faith efforts have been made to trace copyrights on materials included in this publication. If any copyrighted material has been included without permission and due acknowledgment, proper credit will be inserted in future printings after notice has been received.

Printed in the United States of America on acid free paper.

# Dedication

This book is for Bruce, Leah, Katy, Patrick, Gus, Lily, and Jay

# Acknowledgments

*"And now abide faith, hope, love, these three; but the greatest of these is love."*

1 Corinthians 13:13

I am most thankful for my husband, Bruce Gillen, for bringing balance, babies, and bliss into my life.

I am also thankful for my maternal grandparents, Theophilus Brown Flippo and Dora Jane Rasbury Flippo, for planting the seeds of love in my young heart. Without fail, their behavior taught me how to live the good life.

My mother once said to me, "Julie, out of all you three girls, you are the one who loves the most."

And while love should never be a competitive thing, I appreciate her comment, and if it is true, it is because of the nurturing that her own parents gave to me.

I extend my gratitude to Kathy Rhodes for her editorial support in the writing of this book.

I am thankful for the encouragement of my sister, Janey Hickman, and her entire family.

My friends have been a great source of support in my life, and I am most thankful for Timothy Howard Yeager, Chris and Suzanne Fletcher, Bob Duncan, Twyman Towery, Phyllis Gobbell, Doug Jones, Bill Watts, Lori Waltz, Ann Parrish Stevens, Adam Southern, Elizabeth H.

Herndon Potts, Kathie Hicks Fuston, Sheila and Eddie Hickman, Molly Moore Mann, MaryLee Johnson, Rebecca Duncan, Sharon Messick, Dedra Dawson, Sonja and Clark Bennett, Terry and Lynette Sullivan, Jenny Moore, Anne and Bill Draper, Suzette Belvin, Connie Moore, Fannie Wells, Evelyn Mize, LaDelle Smith, and Camille and John Allen.

I appreciate the example that was set by my husband's entire family and the work ethic of his parents, Charlie and Frances Gillen. I also appreciate the support of Ann and Britt Cobb and Bill and Barbara Gillen.

Of course, I am blessed and thankful for our children and grandchildren: Leah, Katy, Patrick, Gus, Lily and Jay.

In 2012, I lost three close friends: William Gay, Michelle Kemper Bottoms, and Mike Gladney. I think about them every day, and I always will.

William Gay was a critically acclaimed writer, but what impressed me most about him was his unconditional love for his children and his complete lack of pretense. I will always appreciate William Gay for his friendship, his support of my writing, and his permission to interview him in March 2004. After William read my first book of columns, *Will the Real Anonymous Mother Please Stand Up?* he said to me, "I didn't know you were so clever." Two days before William died, he wrote a blurb for this book, which also mentioned the word "clever."

It was all because of my maternal great-grandfather, "Pappy" Rasbury, who was mentioned in William's first novel, *The Long Home*, that I met William Gay. And Pappy

Rasbury was the father of my maternal grandmother, who taught me about the authentic components of life.

And so the circle is complete, from Pappy Rasbury to William Gay. They are gone in body, but they will remain in spirit.

Yes, it is true: *"And now abide faith, hope, love, these three; but the greatest of these is love."*

# Table of Contents

**INTRODUCTION** ................................................. xiii

**CLIMBING THE FAMILY TREE** ........................... 1

    My Imaginary World ............................................ 1
    La La Land ........................................................... 3
    Under the Rug ..................................................... 7
    Barbie and Ken .................................................... 9
    Midnight Cowboy ............................................. 11
    Whippoorwills and Daffodils ............................ 13
    Little Patty ........................................................ 16
    Purple Flowers .................................................. 18
    Tree Frogs ......................................................... 20
    Sleep Well, Granny ........................................... 22
    Visions of Sugarplums ...................................... 26
    Cabin Fever ....................................................... 28
    Gus .................................................................... 30
    Vampires ........................................................... 32
    Butter in Tubes ................................................. 35
    Marriage Manual for Young Women ................ 37
    A Fishy Burp .................................................... 40
    Weenie in a Bottle ............................................ 43
    The Adventures of Love Ape ............................ 45
    Cats ................................................................... 47
    My Left Brain ................................................... 49
    Hummus ........................................................... 52
    Be Your Own Vegetable .................................... 54
    What Do You Want on Your Tombstone? ....... 57
    Bacon Wars ....................................................... 59
    Diet Book .......................................................... 62
    Smoking ............................................................ 65
    Lobsters in Cyberspace ..................................... 67
    Waxing Gibbous ............................................... 69

Bedtime Conversations ..................................................... 71
Cleaning My Daughter's House ........................................ 74
Lily .................................................................................... 77

## MEMORY BOULEVARD ........................................... 81

The Zipper ........................................................................ 81
Those Were the Days ....................................................... 84
My Hometown ................................................................. 86
Grapevines ....................................................................... 89
The Student ...................................................................... 91
Girl Scout Trauma ............................................................ 94
"You Did What?" ............................................................. 96
Olga and Helga ................................................................ 98
The Attic ........................................................................ 101
The Lucky Pink Shirt ..................................................... 103
My House Is Right Down That Street ........................... 106
Childhood Girlfriends .................................................... 108
Music, Sweet Music ....................................................... 110
Some Enchanted Evening .............................................. 114
Mamas and Trains .......................................................... 115

## SOUTHERN PRIDE, PREJUDICE, AND RELIGION ................................................................. 119

Hell ................................................................................. 119
The Creature .................................................................. 122
Four Rows of Okra, Part 1 ............................................. 124
Four Rows of Okra, Part 2 ............................................. 128
You Can't Make Me Feel Stoopid Without My Persimmon ..................................................................... 131
Mulletville ...................................................................... 133
Tunica Granny ............................................................... 135
Quilts .............................................................................. 137
Granny ........................................................................... 140
I Like It Like That .......................................................... 142
The Southern Funeral .................................................... 146
The Ten Commandments ............................................... 149
Death vs. Vacation Bible School ................................... 152

Our Father Who Art in School ........................................... 154
Coffee with God ...................................................................... 157
Milk Carton Religion .............................................................. 160
The One That Got Away ........................................................ 162
Inevitability of Miracles ......................................................... 164

# GERITOL MOMENTS ............................................. 169

Moans and Groans ................................................................. 169
Insomnia .................................................................................. 171
Cat Naps .................................................................................. 174
With This Roast I Thee Wed ................................................. 177
To Habit and to Hold ............................................................. 179
Sockies ..................................................................................... 182
Time ......................................................................................... 184
Cicada ...................................................................................... 186
Crunchy Ear ............................................................................ 189
Birthday Tips .......................................................................... 192
Clarity Defined ....................................................................... 194
Fifty Is the New Eighty .......................................................... 197
The Three Dead Dwarfs ......................................................... 199
Masterpieces ........................................................................... 201
Rock Band ............................................................................... 204
Mr. Clean ................................................................................. 206

# HOLIDAY CONFESSIONS ................................... 209

Rabbit, Rabbit ......................................................................... 209
Valentine's Day ....................................................................... 212
Ghostbusters ........................................................................... 214
Halloween Fun ........................................................................ 216
Tasty Bake Oven ..................................................................... 218
Jeggings ................................................................................... 221
Jest 'Fore Christmas ............................................................... 224
Fire ........................................................................................... 227
Lilacs and Petunias ................................................................. 229
Bubbles .................................................................................... 232

# INTRODUCTION

*Under the Rug: Black Lace and Barbie Doll Heads* is a compilation of humor columns that I have written for *The Daily Herald* in Columbia, Tennessee, since July 2000. Many of my columns have also been published in other newspapers and magazines throughout the South and other regions of the country.

    Some of my columns have a Southern bent because I have lived in the South for most of my life. But I am not your typical Southern girl: I am not a Girl Scout Queen or a Cookie-Cutter Cookie. I am a Drop Cookie, fresh-baked, warm and sloppy out of the oven, but still tasty as any Cookie-Cutter Cookie. Perhaps even tastier.

    But being a Southern Drop-Cookie Girl is not required to understand the universal themes of love for home and the land and family roots and religion, but we do at times enhance the beauty therein.

    I understand blackberries on a fence along Highway 43, Rooster Fries, Weenie in a Bottle, Mulletville, and a surprise visit from the preacher while smoking an unladylike Marlboro.

    My audience tells me my columns make them laugh and cry at the same time – and the rebellious Girl Scout Queen/ Drop-Cookie Girl in me likes hearing this, in a mangled sort of way. My loyal readers tell me I am insightful and original, and that I write what everyone else is thinking but would never dare say aloud and this makes me happy because my mama never said any of this stuff to me.

I am a curious girl who has always liked to look under the rug, which is also a metaphor for reading other people's diaries, only to discover that they have written horrible things about me. Warning: You snoop, you discover.

But where are you likely to find real life better than under a rug? Any household rug. Pull up the rug, and you'll find crumbs of daily household truths —the dirt, Legos, tinfoil Hershey wraps, secrets, sins, broken dreams, and Barbie doll heads.

*"Whatever people are ashamed of usually makes a good story,"* F. Scott Fitzgerald said.

People want to read about what's under the rug. I like to sweep it out, expose the reality, and exaggerate it until the truth screams out like an Ape on fire.

I believe I am here to entertain and pierce the heart, but some would say they have no idea why I am here.

So sit back on your sofa, prop up your feet, and read these columns. Maybe you will be inspired to pull up the edge of your own rug and dare to take a peek. It will serve you well, regardless of where you live.

# CLIMBING THE FAMILY TREE

## My Imaginary World

My imaginary world has always been very real to me, but something strange happened in my life, somewhere along the way. The saying, "Be careful what you wish for," is relevant here, because my imaginary world became real. In other words, my writing got published.

In my younger days, I suspected that something along these lines would happen to me, even though I had no ambition other than to play basketball and piano, write notes in school, and chew giant wads of cherry bubblegum until the end of time. I could blow a bubble bigger than my head, and I could blow a bubble within a bubble, and that made me proud.

My mother thought I was crazy when I used to tell her that someday I would be a writer. One day we were on our way to town in the 1968 green Impala, when I announced to her that I would be a writer. She rolled her huge eyes all the way back into her head and said, "Well, hon, what on earth ever gave you that idea? You never even pick up a pencil. Plus, all you ever do is talk on that phone and sit out on the front porch with your feet propped up and watch the cars go by."

And then she lit an L&M and inhaled the whole thing in three seconds, filled the car with smoke, and threw the butt out the window, where an innocent child, or even worse, a stray cat, could have stepped on it. My mother could get arrested for that kind of behavior today. For one thing, I was fourteen years old and she didn't even have me strapped into a car seat, much less a seat belt. Plus, I was the minor child who bought the cigarettes for her.

One night while spying on my parents from behind the kitchen door, I heard my mother say to my father, "Hon, what in the world are we going to do about JULIE? She thinks she is going to be a writer and all she ever does is chew bubblegum and bang on that piano and bounce the basketball up and down five thousand times a day. I do believe she will drive me crazy."

My father did not reply because he was a man and he was not listening.

For some reason, I was unscathed by my parents' lack of confidence in my writing career. Perhaps, it is no coincidence that some of my own children do not embrace my every belief. Suffice it to say that payback has been attained.

Yes, the writing world is glorious indeed. Here are some of the comments I have received from readers through the years, and I will begin with the negative comments first, because it is human nature to yearn for the bad stuff.

Negative comments from readers:
- You are not the Queen of Egypt, but you are the Queen of Denial.
- I wish you would shut up.
- I am glad you get a thrill out of your writing because no one else does.
- I hope the attack scene from Alfred Hitchcock's movie *The Birds* takes place on your front porch.
- You need to have a millstone tied around your neck and be tossed into the ocean in the midst of a hurricane.

Positive comments from readers:
- I like you. You remind me of my grandmother, who died in a ditch by the side of the road after escaping from an insane asylum.
- You looked a lot better with the turban and sunglasses. Put them back on.

Yes, it is a happy life indeed, and I would not have it any other way.

Just remember to be careful what you wish for. Be very, very careful.

## La La Land

Growing up in my family, it didn't matter that things did not make sense. What did matter was what people thought, particularly Mrs. White, the next-door neighbor.

And as is often the case with teenagers, what makes sense to them does not make sense to their parents.

Sure enough, when I hit my teenage years, my father and I were flapping about in the seas of peril over a poster I had hung on my wall. It simply quoted psychotherapist Fritz Perls:

> *You do your thing, and I do my thing*
> *I am not in this world to live up to your expectations*
> *And you are not in this world to live up to mine*
> *You are you, and I am I*
> *Yap yapyap, yap yapyap*
> *And if by chance we find each other*
> *IT'S BEAUTIFUL*

I got home from school one day and discovered my father had removed the poster from my wall. Not only did his behavior seem senseless, it perturbed me greatly. I entered the middle bedroom downstairs, slammed the door, and flung my Nancy Sinatra pointed-toe white go-go boot off my right foot and across the room. It sailed right through the window, leaving shattered glass on the chipped windowsill.

My mother heard the crash and came flying into the bedroom. "Why, Julia Lee! What will Mrs. White think? You march out there and get that go-go boot right now! When your daddy gets home, he's going to hear about this."

The white go-go boot was lying outside the window in the grass. Evidence.

I retrieved the go-go boot and didn't sweat much over my daddy getting home. I'd either cross that bridge when I came to it, or jump out the boot-shaped hole in the window and run and hide in the dogwood tree.

At the time, I wondered why my father removed the poster. It seemed rather mild. Lord knows what he'd have done if he had known my favorite song was "The Pusher" by Steppenwolf. Oh well, I'd just keep that one to myself.

Another daily occurrence that did not make sense was a daily ritual between my mother and her brother. Growing up, my sisters and I witnessed our uncle bursting in on the scene at 717 North Military on a daily basis. He would stalk up the driveway and into the house, invade the kitchen, grab an apple, chomp into it in a way that would make Mr. Ed weep, and he and my mother would stare at each other as he chewed.

It was a strange occurrence. He would only take one or two bites, and then he would put the apple back in the bowl on the table. Then he would pinch or tickle somebody or squirt one of us with water. Finally, he would slink out, slam the back door, and we would watch him saunter back down the driveway and back to his office, which was conveniently located next door.

It was not until May 1997 that I realized we were firmly planted in the heart of La La Land, for La La Land was the only place that senselessness could be tolerated. Back in 1997 I gave La La Land some serious thought, and drew some valid conclusions that still help me today. And while I no longer live in La La Land, I do long for it at least once or twice a day, for there are advantages.

In La La Land, one can eat a whole box of Twinkies and never know it. Only in La La Land do bikinis look fabulous on two-hundred-pound women. Of course, in La La Land women do not weigh two hundred. They weigh one-twenty. In La La Land, Spongebob looks like Don Draper and acts like Billy Graham. There is no such thing as alcoholism, lung cancer is a respiratory infection, suicides are always accidental, and the Pope is going to Hell.

In La La Land, one can get fired and still be in the midst of an enormously successful career. In La La Land, a woman can marry on May first, give birth on May second, and convince herself and her entire family that nine months really have passed.

Immaculate conception occurs frequently in La La Land. There, it is easy to perjure oneself under oath, because the truth is the ultimate weapon in La La Land, and it must be avoided at all costs. In La La Land, no one has any problems whatsoever. Everyone *else* does.

Perhaps the most senseless thing of all in La La Land was that we loved our uncle and he loved us. And if I have learned anything at all, it's that love does not always make sense.

## Under the Rug

Freud claimed the past inhabited the present, and that has certainly been true for me. But what do I see when I look into the future?

I see a young girl with golden hair, maybe ten years old. She is a relative, perhaps a granddaughter or a niece. She is a precocious child, often snuggling up beside me on the couch, asking me questions, searching for clues. And I am a woman older and wiser, in harmony with both myself and my past. I spend time writing and re-reading old books and watering my red geraniums in the clawfoot bathtub, because this is what I want to do.

"Tell me a story," says the girl.

And so I begin. "It was the winter she started putting everything in Mason jars—tea bags, Oreos, vanilla wafers, macaroni shells. After all those years, she'd grown weary of looking at the dust on her piano and feeling sad. One day, she sat on her tapestry sofa in the living room and lifted the rug, staring at the old hardwood floor for a long time. It was at that moment in the cold of January when she realized it was just fine to be the way she was. God's plan, even. Bam! The realization nearly knocked her down. How come no one ever told her this? She sat still and quiet and listened to the language of the air and heard these two words: Remember me.

"But what was under the rug?" asks the girl.

I look down at her and brush back her hair. "Secrets," I say with a serious hush. "Family secrets remanded to be untouched and locked in place. But on that day in January, the woman grabbed a broom and swept the family secrets right out from under the rug and into the naked air, filling it with rage and despair. Neighbors heard the sound of slamming doors and breaking glass and her father singing "Oh How I Love Jesus" on Sunday mornings before church.

Particles of contradiction and inconsistency and paradox flew wild. It was all there, under the rug. Dried up puddles of grief, fake smiles, entire atmospheres of cigarette smoke hovering over strong desire and skeletons of dreams."

"Was there anything good under the rug?" asks the girl.

"Of course. There was cat hair from Sunbeam, the world's greatest cat, and a long-lost gold locket that her grandmother had given her on her sixteenth birthday. There was a Bingo card, a baby tooth, and a faded wedding picture of her parents, and she saved these things for herself."

"Surely, the woman had family," says the girl. "What did they do when she swept out from under the rug?"

"When she told the truth, she ceased to exist. At least to them, anyway. It was hard for her at times. Sometimes, she would look at the cat hair, the baby tooth, the Bingo card, and the picture of her parents and feel a tug at her heart and wipe a tear from her eye, for she could not have it both ways, and yet she did not regret the way she chose."

"But why couldn't she have it both ways?" asks the girl.

"That is how her life was. Sometimes it's like that."

"Was she happy in the end?"

"Yes, very, for in the end, she did not feel like the curtain had closed on the shadow of a life. And she knew there would always be two words there to comfort her—words that no one or no thing could ever steal from her: Remember me."

"Is that all there is?" asks the girl. "Is that the end of the story?"

"Yes," I say.

Content with the ending, I go and water my red geraniums in the bathtub, while the girl curls up with a book and twirls her hair while she reads.

## Barbie and Ken

As a child, I liked to play with Barbie dolls and Easy Bake Ovens. I had no clue at the time, but now I know these toys were camouflaged preparations for my future Betty Crocker role as a wife and mother. Looking back, it's uncanny how my patterns have remained the same: I'd get bored with the Barbie dolls and stuff them naked back into their case, piling all their designer clothes on top of them and flinging them in my closet. Then I'd go whip up a cake or two in my Easy Bake and gobble them down in a couple of swallows, never minding the dishes or any cleanup thereafter.

My mother was tired of a lot of things by the time she had me, so she never said a word about my childhood housekeeping.

Unbeknownst to me, I was still playing house when I married. I was Barbie, and my husband was Ken, and the kitchen was the land of the Easy Bake.

My mother was a far cry from Betty Crocker herself, but there was one commonality: She never acknowledged the existence of sex to my sisters and me. Therefore, I was confused on the night before my wedding, when my mother presented me with a mountain of slinky strapless nightgowns and sexy underwear. It was a rite of passage— a silent ritual-type moment, which I was not to question.

Oh, and I pranced around in and out of the sexy lingerie all right, back in those early days of marriage. I even have a picture of myself in my satin taupe spaghetti-strap gown, lying on the couch with the results of my home pregnancy test, which showed up positive three months after the wedding. A warning to new brides: Be careful while playing house—the Easy Bake Oven can't be stuffed into the garage, and the Barbie doll that you are emulating will come to life and morph into a clueless pregnant woman before you know it. And most importantly, your malleable Ken doll will become stubborn, and he will refuse to play the assigned role in your script.

But if we knew these things back then, we would not marry, just as if we knew what raising teenagers was like, we would never have sex. It's all part of God's plan—

propagation of the species—and it's probably God's greatest source of laughter. You play, you pay.

Things have changed in my marriage. I now sleep in a large gray fleece gown with a polar bear on the front. Like Sleeping Beauty, my Barbie and Ken dolls have been comatose in their case up in the attic for twenty years. I don't cook as much as I used to, and when I do, I clean up the kitchen.

And yet my husband and I are thriving because most of the time we write our own scripts, and they complement each other well. For us, Barbie and Ken were fun for a while, but we're glad they're asleep in the attic, waiting for someone to kiss some life into their lips, if only for a moment.

## Midnight Cowboy

It's that time of year when I think about picking blackberries along the fence row with my cousin, up at our grandparents' farm on Highway 43, right on the edge of town. We'd each have our own pan, and I can still hear the blackberries bouncing when they hit bottom. The two of us would gather enough for a pie, and we'd take them to Granny, and a bubbling cobbler would emerge from her oven in less than two hours. We needed that cobbler to top off the meal of fried green tomatoes, macaroni and cheese, corn, tomatoes, green beans, squash, and cornbread, and some cucumber and onion, and maybe some fried chicken or meat loaf on the side.

Straight from the garden, our grandparents used to say. They were proud of that. After lunch, everyone would scurry back to their places. My grandfather went back to work at his service station, my mother went back home in time to catch *As the World Turns*, and my cousin and I went back outside to walk around the pond or climb the huge maple tree or check out the baby pears on the pear tree in front of the house. Come September, that would be the happening place.

As children, it never occurred to us that things would change. One day the maple tree would be cut down, the pond would be filled, and the house and the pear tree would be uprooted. The garden spot would be paved, and the blackberries would dry up in a field of asphalt.

But let's not get morbid here. For one thing, our grandparents would not like that. They would like to be remembered with the fondness and love that they extended to us. I like to believe that it was enough to carry us through. The house is gone, but the memories remain, and that is enough for me.

Even as a child, I realized the farm was idyllic because of its proximity to town and more specifically, the drive-in. The drive-in was just down the road, extending its arms to people of all ages throughout the town. Typically, the drive-in was a lure for teenage boys and girls, although I did not know that at the time. Carloads of families also piled into the drive-in and consumed popcorn and Cokes to their hearts' content, while staring at the big white screen in the sky.

But one night the drive-in called out to my granny and my aunt, who lived next door. Not your typical drive-in pair, the mother-in-law and the daughter-in-law—Ruth and Naomi out on the town. Let's just say it gave new meaning to the words "whither thou goest."

It was intrigue that sucked them out into the night and beckoned them to drive south down Highway 43 to watch a movie that sounded enticing. Never mind that it was rated X. Never mind that the year was 1969. Never mind that the preacher might see them there. They went anyway, because they liked the title: *Midnight Cowboy*. The rest of us were not there, but we heard the story told through the years, and it was one of our favorites.

Perhaps even the best of gardens, complete with tomatoes, squash, and okra, needs a little spice from time to time, something a tad stronger than pepper and salt.

Here's a toast to summer with all its memories of drive-ins and blackberries, Dustin Hoffman in his early days, and Ruth and Naomi on the prowl.

## Whippoorwills and Daffodils

Cousin Lou called last night, crying.

"What's wrong now?" I asked.

"Ever since the Lynard Skynard band got killed in that plane crash, they just haven't sounded the same."

"That's because they're dead, Lou. Other than being stuck in the '70s, what's really bothering you?" I asked.

"Lately, I've been having a real hard time with leaving and cleaving," she said.

"But you're not even married. Have you been taking your medicine?"

"For about a year now I've been taking the big half of the pill."

"Well, maybe it's time you ate the whole thing. Last time you got like this we had to call the doctor—you were outside talking to Granny, and the only thing out there was the lilac bush."

"Sometimes it bothers me that we have a cousin we never talk to," cried Lou. "Sometimes I just want to call her up and ask, 'How's your life?'"

"Then you should do it if you feel that way," I said. "But I don't feel that way at all. I'm afraid that if I call her up and ask, 'How's your life?' she'll spend the next fifty years telling me."

"But she's our own flesh and blood. She's our cousin."

"She's a parasite posed as a human."

"But don't you miss her?" asked Lou.

"No. I don't miss her at all."

"I'm coming over there," said Lou, sobbing. "Put the coffee on and make sure you have some Cremora Lite."

I have often wondered about the firing patterns of Lou's synapses. She has spent the last five years of her life working on a poem called "Whippoorwills and Daffodils." One minute she'll be singing "Precious Memories," and the next thing you know she'll be talking about the hostage crisis in Iran.

Lou arrived in less than ten minutes and plopped herself down at my kitchen table. "Mama always said there'd come a day when the only thing to get excited about was a bug in the sugar."

"Come on, Lou," I said. "It can't be that bad. At the count of ten, you are going to rise out of your past and step slowly into the present. Ready, set, one, two, three!"

"But they never sang 'The Hallelujah Chorus' at our church," she sobbed.

"Of course not," I said. "It was too uplifting. Four, five, six..."

"I'm not in the mood for this year," said Lou. "I'd like to lay my head down on your kitchen table and cry for five days."

"No hair on my kitchen table," I said. "Seven, eight, nine..."

"How come people lived to be so old back in Bible days?" asked Lou.

"They couldn't count," I said.

"Do you think I'll ever finish "Whippoorwills and Daffodils?" she asked.

"No. I think whippoorwills and daffodils will become extinct before you ever finish that poem. TEN! You are now in the present!"

"But what is my purpose in life?" cried Lou.

"Enjoy your coffee while it's still hot," I said. "That's all any of us can do."

"I'll drink to that," said Lou. "Will you pass me that Cremora Lite?"

## Little Patty

*"For in much wisdom is much grief: and he that increaseth knowledge increaseth sorrow."*

—King Solomon (Ecclesiastes 1:18)

I am sure that if my mother opened my book, she would slam it and scream.

It's almost Mother's Day, and of course I think about my mother every year on this day, not only because of the holiday but because her birthday was also in May, and her pink and red and purple and white impatiens and petunias were bursting from her white flower boxes in May. That was back before she became obsessed with wood ferns.

I think May was my mother's favorite month, but it's hard to tell because she was an enigma. The more I looked for answers to my questions, the more black holes I fell into, so I just gave up and wrote a book. But a recent e-mail from my sister's friend who lived behind us and spent a lot of time at our house put a new spin on an old theme, otherwise known as my mother. She wrote:

"I have been reading your book tonight, looking for memories, and I found them. I loved your mother so much. I always think of her and look for her white car in the driveway. I will never forget her sitting on the stool in the kitchen, smoking, and drinking coffee, looking out the kitchen window, but I never knew she was looking out for your grandfather.

"Nobody will ever say good grief or good night like Little Patty—that was what we sometimes called your mother. She had the best laugh.

"I had forgotten about Thomasina, but I do remember her. And Tinkerbell—what a little princess. When I had my daughter in 1979, that summer, I wanted Little Patty to see her. She was alone, and we talked about Tinkerbell. And we talked about her girls—she was kind of proud of them."

When I first heard from the neighbor, I was struck by the mention of Tinkerbell, the white toy poodle, before the mention of my sisters and me. Corroborating evidence indeed. I swear that dog had a diamond tiara that my mother pulled out of the closet and placed on Tinkerbell's head every day after we left for school.

The friend went on to write, "Little Patty had a wicked and charming laugh rolled up into one that I would love to hear again. Maybe someday when we all get up there, she'll have Tinkerbell in her arms, trying to give her some smooches, wearing some old shoes that she just slides into, telling her girls to grab a handful of clean clothes on their way up the stairs, and making one of her faces."

Again, right on target. I was always making my mother roll her eyes and make faces, but I was laughing every step of the way. For example, she never forgave me for the time I wore the T-shirt that said, "Get Really

Stoned. Drink Wet Cement," and ran smack-dab into the preacher at the post office. Boy, have I paid for that one.

And just when I had come to believe I was no longer capable of being grabbed by anything on earth, the neighbor went on to ask a question that grabbed me hard. She asked, "Was Patty ever impressed with anybody?"

Well, I never really thought about that before, but I have thought about it a lot in the last two weeks. I think my mother was somewhat impressed with Lisa and Kim on *As the World Turns*, but it bothered her that they, too, were flawed. Looking back, I think the only thing that impressed her was a good cup of coffee.

And you know what? I'm beginning to feel the same way.

## Purple Flowers

My mother's purple irises are blooming, mixed in with the lavender yarrow she gave me the last time I saw her. It was eighteen years ago in May, and I'd stayed with her for a week while my husband was out of town. We had a garden that year, and I had to get back to my own house and check on things. Before I left, my mother dug up some purple iris bulbs and mounds of lavender yarrow, which I took home and planted in my yard.

We had strawberries in our backyard garden that year—my husband says the first year is always the best, and he was right. Everything was thriving that year—I was pregnant once again, the strawberries were sweet and red, the blackberries were blooming, and my mother's irises and yarrow took quickly to new ground.

But ripe fruit soon spoils. The irises and the yarrow and I continued to spread, but my mother died with the strawberries. Now, eighteen years later, the child I gave birth to continues to grow, and the irises and the yarrow still spread throughout the ground in which they were planted.

The yarrow is prolific, and last year my husband became so exasperated he doused it with Roundup. "Don't poison my mother!" I yelled.

"Your mama is doing all right," he said. And he's right. Oh, I don't know that for sure, but I feel it in my heart, and her lavender yarrow signifies she's still around, keeping an eye on things and making sure she's not forgotten. Sometimes I go out there and douse it with a cup of coffee and toss it a cigarette. I've spread it all over the yard and given cuttings to friends and family, and they report she's doing well in their yards, too.

This year she's stronger than ever, and my husband has given up. Inwardly I chuckle, because I know that if she had lived, he would have surrendered and laid down his bottle of Roundup.

My mother had a way of taking over without even trying, a way of spreading herself around her daughters and her friends in an inexplicably attractive manner. She was accommodating and funny, and she kept her secrets to herself. We never noticed this until she died, because we were too busy talking about ourselves. But in looking back, one of my mother's strongest appeals was that she never said anything about herself. She just listened and laughed, often maniacally, about our own predicaments, and it was a comfort that we have all missed more than we ever would have imagined.

A few years ago, I visited Rowan Oak, the home of William Faulkner. Renovation was underway, and I stuck a couple of loose iris bulbs in my pocket. When I got home, I planted them in a big clay flowerpot with my mother's lavender yarrow, and now they are both in bloom—shades of purple, side by side. Next year I'll plant them in the ground where they can quietly spread, free and wild.

They're happier that way.

## Tree Frogs

My great-grandmother died at age ninety-three, when I was in sixth grade, and I was distraught, because I do not like goodbyes, and I have spent significant and creative portions of my life attempting to avoid the "acceptance" phase of death. Oh, I haven't stuffed a toy poodle or enclosed anyone in a glass coffin and placed it smack dab in the middle of the parlor, but I do have a hard time with goodbyes.

When my great-grandmother died, my mother was also distraught for the usual reasons, among them, what I was going to wear to the funeral. Her exact words as she cranked up a fresh pot of coffee and fired up an L&M were, "Gad! What in the world is Julie going to wear to the funeral?" But we went to Dooley's and bought three dresses in about ten minutes, and I have a vague recollection of a pale blue-striped cotton that somehow had "seventh-grade" written all over it.

I had only been to one other funeral, back when I was in third grade and my mother quickly realized she should have informed me that people died and did not return in the form to which we were accustomed. In other words, they would not walk back through the front door, grab a Coke out of the fridge, plop down in a chair, and say, "How you doin'?"

In the midst of my first funeral, this reality struck me so hard that my tears turned into a snot-filled blubber, the kind that made people look and lean and become highly intrigued. Meanwhile, my mother started gouging me with her elbow and whispering things in my ear, things like, "Hush that mess up right now and hold your breath and count to five hundred and we'll get out of here soon. Think about a white kitten." And then she sat up straight with an attempt at great dignity and pride in her daughter, but I blubbered till the end of the service and on into the night.

The years that passed between third grade and seventh grade bestowed upon me a tad of maturity and understanding of goodbyes, and I made it through my great-grandmother's funeral until they sang "When They Ring Those Golden Bells." Still, there was no blubber or snot, and after the burial we all went up to our grandparents' house to sit around and talk and eat and visit with each other.

It was all very normal until the tree frogs came. Suddenly, and without warning, tiny tree frogs invaded the side door entry, and a few of them hopped inside the house and my grandmother said, "Good Lord, she's come back!"

There was great surprise and laughter, and a certain comfort filled the air and remained in my heart. Until that day, tree frogs had never appeared at the door and hopped into the house. Perhaps we will never know why they came to visit at that particular time, but I like to believe they came to reveal to us that the deceased often do walk back through that front door in various forms, and give us something to talk about and think about and hope for, because they knew we would need it.

Somehow the tree frogs made the "acceptance" phase a lot easier for me, and I am thankful for their mystery and their presence.

## Sleep Well, Granny

I had the best grandmother in the world, and although she died in 1982, I still think of her often. In all my years with her, she never criticized me a single time. In fact, I never heard her criticize anyone at all. How did she manage to do this? I'm not sure. All I know is she was a happy person, full of contentment, and she was a joy to all who knew her.

One of Granny's secrets to life was going to bed whenever she felt the need. She often took a short nap around ten in the morning, right after *Concentration*, and later she'd nap in the afternoon, dozing off to the theme song of *Guiding Light*. I've been told Granny stayed in bed for a week after my mother announced her plans to marry my father, and I've come to believe Granny had the right idea all along.

When Granny was diagnosed with cancer in 1982, she hit the bed, smiling all the while and pretending she was just resting. "When I get better," she'd say, "We'll drive out to California and see the Pacific." Not once did she complain of feeling bad, and not once did she mention the word "cancer." Some would call it denial, but I call it Granny's Way. She knew she was dying, but what good would it do to talk about it? Words didn't cure lung cancer, and she knew it.

A large part of my life with Granny was spent in the kitchen, "helping" her cook. She was a wonderful cook, and she did everything the old-fashioned way. I can still see her holding a coconut in her left hand and whacking it with a small claw hammer in her right hand, then peeling and grating the coconut and turning it into a three-layer cake that could have graced any cover of *Southern Living*. A summer meal at Granny's house was spectacular, and she took pride that everything was fresh from the garden, picked that very day: green beans, corn, tomatoes, squash, cucumbers, okra, the works. As Granny and I cooked in her kitchen, we could look straight out the window and see the garden in all its glory, and it is only now that I appreciate it fully.

Food was central to our lives, and in the latter stages of Granny's illness, I became convinced I could save her with food. One night my sister and I were up at her house, Granny's bald head wrapped in a blue turban. It was late October and dark outside, and we were sitting around the kitchen table we'd feasted at all our lives. But in the end there was no jubilee: Granny had no appetite anymore, and for the first time in my life, she was skin and bones. The corset she'd worn all her life would have fallen to the floor if she'd been able to put it on.

That night I scrambled her some eggs and became ecstatic when she ate them, like a new mother whose firstborn had just swallowed the first glob of strained carrots. "Granny is going to live!" I proclaimed. Every little sign turned into hope. Thus the fate of the eternal optimist.

The next day Granny slipped into a coma, from consciousness to unconsciousness, just like that.

The night Granny died I was talking long distance to my soon-to-be husband on the phone when I got the beep. It was the early days of call waiting, and my father was on the other end. "She's gone," he said, and I hung up the phone and stood behind the rocking chair, alone in my apartment. In the stillness, I felt a calm presence sweep across me. To this day I believe it was Granny, dropping in to comfort me as she had all of my life.

I went up to my grandparents' house, and the hearse had already carried her body away. My mother was there, along with my father and my drunk uncle and his wife, who quickly proceeded to gather Granny's linens and began dispersing them among the grandchildren.

My mother's cowardice was stretched to the hilt, and she screamed, "Daddy's not dead yet! Those are his!" It was a predecessor of days to come, though I did not know it then. Things unfold in their own time, I have learned.

During Granny's illness, my mother gained twenty pounds because she ate to compensate for the food her mother could no longer eat. And after Granny's death, my mother began to cook like her, in a seeming attempt to bring her back to life.

Although my own children never met my grandmother, she lives on. She's there in the roast and carrots and potatoes, the fried corn and fresh tomatoes and green beans. She's there on the couch taking a nap during the day, and late at night she's sitting up on the couch working her crossword puzzles as the trucks fly down Highway 43 in the distance.

With wonder, she's reading everything from the Bible to *Beowulf*. Granny once told me, "I can go all over the world right here on my couch, with a book in my hands."

Sleep well, Granny.

## Visions of Sugarplums

It's the holiday season, that glittery time of year when our visions of sugarplums and togetherness sometimes dance out of our heads and smash head-on into a tree of reality.

I once wrote a column called "One of These Days," in which I spoke of things I will do in my life—tasks decided, yet unfinished. I mentioned writing monthly letters to my children, teaching the concept of grace to future grandchildren, and driving down Highway One and staring at the Pacific.

In the midst of my sugarplum moment, I was also blindsided by this fantasy of reconciliation with a relative. I wrote:

"And I might try to reconcile with a relative. I'll make a fresh blackberry cobbler like my grandmother used to make and give it to that relative with whom I have reconciled. Maybe we'll sit down and eat it together, piled high with vanilla ice cream and disregard for calories, cholesterol, and the past. Maybe we can look at the big picture and both sides of the coin together, and walk on in a path of acceptance. One of these days, these things will happen. Perhaps, I'll buy some fresh blackberries today."

I visited the relative because it seemed like a good idea at the time. Yet, if Elizabeth Barrett Browning were alive today, she could have molded my sugarplum moment into another poem called "How Can I Reject Thee? Let Me Count the Ways."

And if I wrote a book about visiting the relative, here are some possible titles:

- *When I Extended the Olive Branch, She Used It to Roast Marshmallows*
- *Maybe and Perhaps: Two Words My Relative Does Not Want to Learn*
- *My Relative Does Not Wish to Eat My Blackberry Cobbler*
- *My Relative Prefers to Look at the Small Picture, One Side of the Coin, and Live in a World Where the Sky Is Green and the Grass Is Blue*
- *Dreams of a Sugarplum Fairy: Still Waiting for My Relative to Wake Up from Her Long Winter's Nap*
- *My Relative is from Mars; I am from Venus and Headed to Jupiter*

Bitter, you ask? Nah. Not me. Oh, I was temporarily dismayed and taken aback by the rejection, and then I kicked myself for thinking it could ever be any different. But I live in a world with green grass and blue skies. I'm just a girl who comes from a family that prefers denial over reconciliation, and lies over truth, all in the name of saving face.

A wise man once told me, "It's always OK to let people know you care." That's all I was trying to do with my relative, and I do not regret the visit that crashed me into reality.

I love the truth, and I value it above all else in life. Luckily, this world is full of people who embrace the words "perhaps" and "maybe," and who would gladly accept my blackberry cobbler.

I'll go visit them next time.

## Cabin Fever

The global warming effect dumped three inches of snow on us, and here we are in a winter wonderland. My tendency to hole up and snuggle down reminds me of Robert Frost's poem, "Stopping by Woods on a Snowy Evening."

But I have promises to keep, and bills to pay before I sleep. Or something like that.

Yes, I'd love to hunker down in my feather bed until the Ides of March, but I have children and cats, all howling with hunger and ripping the furniture to shreds.

The snow has bonded us in ways we will remember, ways we will yearn for in mid-July and in the snowless days of next winter.

We've played Spades, and we've played Monopoly. We've watched reruns of *The Andy Griffith Show* and *The Twilight Zone*. We've eaten snow cream and built snowmen, and we've stared into the crackling fire for many an hour.

We've taken long naps and long baths, and we've drunk hot chocolate and read some good books. We have watched football.

This is winter at its best, and I am thankful.

Somehow the snow makes the coffee seem hotter and the bed seem warmer. Perhaps I am reminded that I could be outside rather than inside, but by the grace of God, I am not.

I remember the New Year's snow of 1963. My family and I were among a large gathering of close friends on that fateful night. As the story goes, it began to snow deep into the heart of a serious Pinochle game. The grown-ups were huddled around the kitchen table, smoking cigarettes and laughing raucously, as close friends do.

All the kids were huddled around the TV in the den, watching *The Andy Griffith Show* and *The Twilight Zone*. There were eighteen people in that house: eight adults and nine kids, and a three-week-old baby girl.

After the card game ended, and after "Auld Lang Syne" was sung, we were shocked to step outside into an unprecedented mountain of snow. When did this happen? Our Volkswagen was buried in a snowdrift. Huge billows and tufts of snow were piled up in the road, and there was no way we could get back home. All eighteen of us ended up spending the night there under one roof. The next morning, we ate a huge breakfast of bacon, eggs, sausage, and pancakes. Miraculously, there was plenty of food.

We all stayed warm and we all stayed dry and we all stayed fed, among friends. It simply doesn't get any better than that.

The next day we were able to drive home, but we talked about that snowy New Year's Eve surprise for years.

Yesterday, I called up my old family friend to reminisce about the New Year's snow of 1963. She had been thinking about it, too. Out of those eighteen people, two of the best are no longer with us—her husband and my mother. How nice it would be to see them once more, huddled around that kitchen table, slapping their Pinochle cards down in the obliviousness of the snow.

Those were the days, and these are the days.
Let's get cozy and make them count.

## Gus

When my first child left for college, I fretted and cried and wrung my hands for twelve months prior to graduation. After she left, I spent the week in mourning with her baby book in one hand and a bag of Snickers in the other, while my heart fell to my knees. For my first child, I wrote a column titled "From Blue to Green."

When my second child left for college, I considered actually going back to college and rooming with her, like Rodney Dangerfield in *Back to School*, but she was opposed to the idea. So we bought fun stuff for her new dorm room, and when we drove her away and dropped her off at the doorstep, my heart fell to my feet. I can still see her standing there with those great big puppy-dog eyes, and for my second child, I wrote a column titled "Change of Venue."

When my third child left for college, my heart was somehow back in place. By that time I had begun to learn that life goes on when our hearts do not, and I had become a more practical woman. He drove off into his future with a microwave, a cell phone, a computer, and two sets of those extra-long twin bed sheets that they use in dorms. As he drove away, I wiped a tear from my eye, then went into his bedroom and jumped up and down on his bed. For my third child, I wrote a column titled "Neptune."

My fourth child leaves for college this Saturday, and I am writing a column titled "I'm Glad I Had That Surgery a While Back." My heart is intact, or at least it has been until this moment of truth when I see the words in black and white appear before my eyes—the ones that spell out, "He is leaving." Ouch. Suddenly, I am having an end-of-an-era moment, and my heart is going pitter-pat, because this child's a sweetie.

This is Gus, the child who was named after Texas Ranger Augustus McCrae in *Lonesome Dove*, because we watched that movie over and over during the winter of 1991, when he was on his journey into this world. Like many *Lonesome Dove* fans, we still watch that movie over and over, and we sometimes recite the lines, such as Captain Woodrow F. Call's classic, "Better to have it and not need it than need it and not have it."

It is truly different the fourth time around. The heart is older and wiser and does not drop to the ground as easily as it did in the younger days of parenthood. Still it is there, full of love and memories and thanks for this last child of ours. I think of all that has transpired between the first child and the last child—things like X-Box 360 and Vitamin Water and digital cameras and Twitter. Things like heartbreak and perseverance and declaring a major and trying to decipher what is good and what is true in this world.

I don't know what I will do when the last one leaves home. As my husband says, "The nest may be empty, but the birdhouse is full on weekends."

Good luck, Gus. We'll leave the light on.

## Vampires

Have my children turned into vampires? It seems that three out of four of them are sleeping during most of the waking hours. Have they watched *True Blood* on demand just a few times too many? And if they sleep all day, what are they doing at night? The thought of it makes me shudder, and yet I do not lose any sleep over it because I like to sleep at night, and so does my husband. In fact, plopping into our bed each night has become our favorite thing to do.

In this stressful world in which we live, it's nice to know there is that one period within the twenty-four-hour span that we are unconscious and unaware of the boogeyman, the taxman, and the occasional demented mailman. Until we start having nightmares, that is. I'll admit, my nightmares would make Freddy Krueger run and scream for his mama and leap up into her lap while sucking his mangled thumb. My nightmares are so creepy that Freud and Jung would have stuffed me in a cage and turned me into a human lab rat. My nightmares make vampires look like a clip of Bert and Ernie baking a batch of lemon squares for Miss Piggy.

Yes, vampires are very much in vogue these days, and it's possible that my children are among them. Child #1 does not sleep in. It appears she inherited a strong work ethic that would astound Paul Bunyan. Child #2 not only sleeps in, but takes naps along the way. Upon waking, her classic line while yawning and stretching is, "I'm so tired."

Child #3 likes to sleep in, and he will not budge or speak for at least one hour after he assumes a sitting position with coffee in hand. He also goes through a ritualistic moping phase in which he will grimace and groan and exude sheer disgust at the mention of getting up, taking a shower, or brushing his teeth.

Child #4 has also become a sleeper, which has contributed to his summer school status. I'll text him and ask, "Are you awake?"

He'll text back, "No, I had a busy night, and I'm just sleeping in today. I don't really need to go to that Differential Equations class anyway."

I'll pick up the phone and ask, "Isn't that the reason you're in summer school in the first place? From sleeping in just a little too often?"

"Bye, Mom," he'll say. "I'll call you when I wake up."

In all fairness, he is passing the class, which apparently requires eighteen hours of sleep and an endless supply of Cheese Nips.

Child #2 has had my car all summer, and I want it back, so I text her to make arrangements.

"I'm thinking I might get my car today or you could bring it Saturday. Which do you prefer?"

"Saturday," she replies. "I will be asleep tomorrow morning."

A couple of weeks ago I texted Child #3, "Today is Father's Day."

"I know," he replies. "I'll get him some golf balls when I wake up. And a card and maybe a golf glove." Big tiger yawn and groan here. "Call me later, Mom, I'm sleeping."

Maybe they'll outgrow it. That's all a mother can wish for, if they want to have any kind of future that involves a paycheck. Meanwhile, I remind myself that the early bird catches the worm, as I march on in my original biorhythmic form of waking at five in the morning and saying things to my husband such as, "The Vernal Equinox occurs today."

Of course, the downside of waking at five every morning is going to sleep at seven each night. While my husband is out in the den watching *Swamp Men* and screaming, "Shoot him! Shoot him!" in Cajun talk, the phone will ring for me, and he will urge me to speak to a solicitor of goodwill that always involves money or volunteer work. I've learned to roll over and say to my husband, "Tell 'em I'll save a duck or cure malaria or something like that. I'm not talking to anybody till five in the morning."

Works every time.

## Butter in Tubes

I recently conducted a pet peeve survey among a random group of people, otherwise known as my family. I sat prim and proper in a chair in the den, yellow legal pad and pen in hand and asked, "What is your biggest pet peeve?"

The silence was deafening. I looked at all of them and there they sat, just staring at ME, of all people. "Why are you all looking at me?" I asked. "Surely you all have at least one thing that grates on your nerves so rawly that you want to fling it off the deck, over the pine trees, and into the park. Come on, what is it?"

The youngest spoke first, as the youngest will so often do. "I hate it when you ask me if I brushed my teeth every morning on the way to school. And I'm sick of you asking if I want an orange Tic Tac."

I take notes in silence, without looking at the little imp. "Next," I say. Again there is silence, and I notice my daughters are looking at each other with that "should we or shouldn't we?" look on their faces. "Spit it out," I say. "There's nothing you can say that will shock me any more than car insurance rates, college tuition, parking tickets on campus, or the cost of textbooks these days."

The younger daughter speaks. "I hate it when you tell about the time you woke up at a slumber party in eighth grade and decided to invent butter in tubes. I'm sick of hearing about how you woke all your friends up and screamed, 'They should invent butter in tubes!' and how you wrote the Parkay company and they rejected your idea and a few months later they came out with squeezable margarine. I'm sick of it, just sick of it. If I ever hear that story again, I am going to scream."

"I had forgotten all about that!" I exclaim. "Thank you for reminding me! Do you realize it has been YEARS since I awoke with the idea of putting butter in tubes? I still cannot believe they rejected my idea, then had the audacity to come out with the squeeze version a few months later. The nerve of them!"

I fling the yellow legal pad onto the dining room table and kick off my St. Patrick's Day flip-flops, and through the fog in my brain, I somehow notice that my entire family is staring at me, even my husband.

The third child speaks. "I hate it when you wear your St. Patrick's Day flip-flops after St. Patrick's Day. "Why don't you wear your pink flip-flops?"

I used to like this child because he always said "thank you" after each and every meal I cooked for him. How quickly things change. "Did you ever see the movie *Alien*?" I ask him. "The first one, where the alien bursts from the belly of the fembot? That's what it was like when you were born. I'll wear my St. Patrick's Day flip-flops all the way to Kingdom Come if I feel like it."

By now, all the children are snickering and muttering something about the word "fembot," and how it did not originate from the *Alien* movie. My husband looks at all of us and says, "That's enough. This is not working." And then he gets up and turns up the TV because there is an exciting show on about ground walnut shells and the plot is thickening fast.

The children are still giggling, and I pick up my yellow legal pad and put on my flip-flops and regain my dignity and walk out of the den. My mind drifts back to my eighth-grade year and the night I awoke with the idea that they should put butter in tubes, and I am thankful for my second daughter's pet peeve and how she reminded me of my shining moment.

Butter in tubes seemed like a good idea at the time, and somehow it still does.

## Marriage Manual for Young Women

Since my husband and I have been married for twenty-nine years, the thought occurred to me just this morning that I am well-qualified to provide an instruction manual for soon-to-be brides. Oh sure, I could be burning up mismatched socks in the fireplace or feather-dusting the cats, but this will be of much more benefit to young women who are about to tie the knot with their beloved.

Perhaps the first thing they need to know is there are many ways to tie knots, but since I was never a Boy Scout, I do not know the actual names of the knots. I have just learned how to creatively tie them through trial and error, and I am here to help and serve these young women along the winding paths of their marital experience.

Sweeties, I am going to be honest here. I see the basking glows in your wedding announcements in the paper, and I myself recall those early days of young love with all its adoring stares, glances, and the sweetness and lure of the passion flower.

Young marital love is a sweet, sweet love that will pale only in comparison to the feelings you will experience upon seeing your newborn baby for the very first time, and believe me, this event can follow the wedding vows very quickly, depending on the maturity level and the planning skills and the judgment of the new bride.

In my case, I somehow gave birth to four babies before I had written the last thank-you note for the wedding gifts, but for now, let's keep the focus off of my experience and benefit from my complete lack of conscious thought during those early days. I will say that I have no regrets whatsoever and it was not my fault that I found my husband irresistible. It was not I who gave him those baby blue eyes or any of his other fine attributes.

For starters, you need to at least be vaguely aware that at some point in your marital future, there will be times when you will utter the following words to your husband:

"You want me to do WHAT?"

"How did my hand end up here?"

\* \* \*

Later on down the road, you will have a conversation that goes like this, in regard to the home theatre your hubby has installed in your Better Homes and Gardens living room:

You will say, "Let's turn that thing off so we can talk."

He will say, "What do you want to talk about?"

"I don't know . . . last night, maybe," you will say.

"Thought we done talked about that," he will say, flicking the remote with a glazed look in his eye, after not once gazing into your eyes.

"Why don't you ever gaze into my eyes anymore?" you will ask. And then you will start sniffling lightly, then crying gently, and move on into waves of grief and despair, with a box of Kleenex in hand (this is important), while you pathetically wipe up your giant puddles of tears off of the floor.

At this point he will turn the volume down, and he may even look at you. Even if he does not make eye contact with you, he will ask, "Honey, what's wrong? What do you want me to do?"

"I WANT TO MOVE TO A TROPICAL ISLAND!" you will scream at the exact volume in which Tom Cruise screamed "Show me the money!" in the movie *Jerry McGuire*.

Coincidentally, this is the same manner in which Katie Holmes is now screaming to Tom: "What was I thinking when I married you? I can't be a Scientologist—I DESERVE to take drugs while giving birth to our next baby! How was I to know you would turn out to be nothing but a mutant toothy creation of L. Ron Hubbard?"

Yes, there will be times when you will turn into a screaming banshee, and the content of your messages will be directly proportionate to your age and the ages of your children and how you react when you realize that Acai

Berry is just another flat-tummy scam, like that Smash-o-Burger you bought from an infomercial in an attempt to be the efficient role model of the perfect housewife.

In short, here are my thoughts regarding the future young brides of today: Sometimes it's OK to say yes, sometimes it's OK to say no, and sometimes it's OK to act on complete and unabashed impulse.

Whatever paths you choose, may your love grow sweet and strong, throughout the storms of life, and may you embrace and relish these tender days of the sweet and clueless innocence of your youth.

Love may not always build a bridge, but it will always find a way.

## A Fishy Burp

While government research and funding run rampant, we will be bankrupt and dead by the time conclusive results are in concerning the recommended daily amount for Omega 3. Meanwhile, the American Dietetic Association and the American Heart Association both advocate two servings of fatty fish per week.

We are told that salmon is the best source, followed by herring and sardines.

Salmon, no problem. Herring? I'll try it. Sardines? Well, my grandfather ate them, and if they were good enough for him, they're good enough for me. To be perfectly honest here, I'm lying. I'd eat my Christmas tree before I would eat a sardine. Sorry, Bampy.

"But what about the mercury intake of fish?" cry hungry hordes of five-hundred-pound Americans. "We can't risk our health and expose ourselves to mercury!"

We are once again assured by a government expert that the health benefits of fish far outweigh the risks of mercury intake.

What's the big deal here? When our first baby was born, we feared that she had a fever. Rather than call 9-1-1, my husband suggested we take her temperature. But what if the thermometer is WRONG?" I cried.

"Well, why don't you just stick it into that cup of spiced tea and see how hot it is?" he suggested. How was I to know he was being sarcastic?

And so I stuck the thermometer into my spiced tea, and like a young woman awaiting the results of her home pregnancy test, I stared at the thermometer and jerked it out after I could wait no more. Suddenly, I noticed many tiny silver balls rolling across our kitchen floor.

"What's that?" I asked, noticing that when I poked them they would split and form more tiny balls.

"It's MERCURY!" my husband screamed. "Get it out of here!"

And so I took the broom and swept it clear out the door and onto the neighbors' grass. That was twenty-five years ago and we're still here. Not sure about the neighbors.

It is important not to be overly minimalistic here, because there are true mercury risks with certain species of fish. Sharks, for instance, contain high levels of mercury, so remember: Don't eat the shark that bites you.

As with any quest for truth, the more we read about the benefits and risks of fish, the more confused we become in the process. There is a solution, however, and it is a simple one. Take a fish supplement! Pop a fish pill and down a Twinkie!

But alas, there is yet another concern: Fish Burp. Is this not the sexiest thing you have ever heard of in your life? There is great potential here for men and women alike. Lines such as, "Not tonight honey . . . you have (whisper) fish burp." Then a soft kiss on the forehead will soothe any hurt feelings.

This is true—we are likely to experience an unpleasant aftertaste known as "fish burp" after ingesting fish oil pills. What's a wanna-be health nut to do? Fear not! You can freeze your fish-oil pills to mitigate your fish burp and all will be well.

So go pop that frozen fish-oil pill and inhale that Twinkie and guzzle that Sundrop and enjoy the benefits of mercury-free Omega 3 while waiting for the government results to roll in a hundred years from now.

Just sit back in your recliner, turn on the ballgame, and remember to grab a platter of mile-high nachos and the remote.

## Weenie in a Bottle

Have you ever noticed that women are exploited more through language than men are? Think about it. In a previous column, I wrote about two new products for women—"Bigger Bust" and "Liposuction in a Bottle." Other than being blatant lies, these product names leave little to the imagination.

Men's products are different. Take Cialis, for instance. "Cialis" sounds like some kind of high-energy carrot juice drink, or perhaps a new cologne. The name has a certain mystique and even a hint of dignity about it. Why? Why don't they call Cialis "Weenie in a Bottle?" Why isn't Rogaine called "Hair Up There?" Why do women get all the cutesy names?

"Hooters" is another good example. My husband tried to get me to eat at Hooters once, but I refused.

"Let's go eat at Hooters," he begged, crawling across the floor on all-fours with a rose clinched between his teeth. "I heard the fries were really good."

"I'll go eat at Hooters when you go eat at Peckers," I said.

"That place shut down," he snickered. "All the peckers hung out over at Hooters."

Truth is, if they had a "Peckers," women would torch the place.

There is a basic difference between men and women. It's called supply and demand.

Consider the infinite world of women's underwear. Victoria's Secret alone has countless garments that are linguistically creative. Flip through a catalog, and you'll find The Miracle Bra, The Natural Miracle Bra, Dream Angels, Body Bare V-Strings, and The Body Bare Collection. Glance at the Internet, and you'll discover the Wonder-Packed-Padded-Gel Bra, Wonderform, and more slinky wonder-lures than you care to imagine. And, of course, we still have old standards like Playtex Living Bras and Playtex Cross Your Heart Bras. I wonder what these names were intended to convey. Live mammalian tissue? Honesty? These bras are products of the Fifties. Back then, were women perceived to be untrustworthy vixens with dead boobs?

Men don't have a Victoria's Secret equivalent. They have Hanes and Fruit of the Loom, and they seem perfectly content. It's not fair, but they don't care.

The fragrance world is also unbalanced. Women's perfumes sound exotic and sexy. Pick a splash and transform into "Caesar's Woman," "Baby Doll," or "Oh! De Moshino."

Women's fragrances are categorized in three ways: Designer names, like "Gucci," French names, like "L'Air Du Temps," and powerful one-word names, such as "Delicious" and "Feelings." There's even one called "Iceberg." Now there's a good line: "Not tonight, baby—I'm wearing Iceberg."

Today's man has more variety than Old Spice and Brut, but the language of men's fragrance is much less evocative than women's.

Men's fragrances include colors, like "Dark Blue" and "d'Orange." He may douse himself with a number, such as "212," "273," or "4711." If he's really feeling frisky, he can mist himself with "Alabama." Your man may also dab "Unleaded," "Boss," or "What About Adam" behind his ears, so look out. He may slap on some "Casino," "Joops," or my personal favorite, "PinoSylvestre."

Actually, I've never gotten a whiff of "PinoSylvestre," but it sure sounds safer than "Eau Sauvage," "Samba Natural Man," or "Cigar."

Freud said, "Sometimes a cigar is just a cigar."

And sometimes it's a lot more.

## The Adventures of Love Ape

My husband has turned into Love Ape.

There I was, all snuggled and cozy underneath my soft down comforter, when suddenly I was awakened by the primate formerly known as Carl.

"Love Ape lonely," he said, with a pouty lip.

"What?" I asked, grabbing my glasses.

"Love Ape lonely," he repeated, and the next thing I knew I was in the clutches of Love Ape's warm embrace.

"Love Ape like," he said with a smile.

I had to admit, this was pretty cute. And besides, it offered potential. Think of the advantages of having a man who would only utter three-word sentences, such as "Love Ape lonely," and "Love Ape like." There would be no more political banter, rational discussions about money, or decisions about the kids. All I would have to do is keep Love Ape happy, and he would be good.

"What would Love Ape like?" I asked. "A banana?"

"No, Love Ape not like banana. Love Ape like *you*."

"OK, Love Ape. Just shut up and turn out the light and we'll see what we can work out here."

The next morning I was awakened to the wild monkey-like sound of Love Ape's bliss.

"Love Ape happy," he said. "Love Ape love you."

Now tell me, who could resist this? The birth of Love Ape had truly presented a delightful turn in our marriage.

"I love Love Ape," I said, patting him on the head and wondering if this was healthy.

"Love Ape turn out light?" he asked.

"No, Love Ape . . . it's morning. The lights won't turn out, and I have to make the coffee now."

"Love Ape like coffee," he said.

I was getting a little concerned at this point. Love Ape's sentences had grown into four and five words, and my attraction to the single digit IQ primate was waning. I tucked him back under the covers and slipped out of the bedroom, closing the door behind me.

Ten seconds later he was leaping down the hall, beating his chest, and grinning from ear-to-ear. "Love Ape cold! Love Ape need blankie!" he said, grabbing me.

"Look, Love Ape," I said. "You're cute and all, but I like a man who's just a little more civilized from time to time. You know, someone who can discuss politics and help me make decisions about money and the kids."

"Love Ape read newspaper," he said wiping a fake tear from his eye. "You not love Love Ape anymore."

"Oh, come on, Love Ape," I said, feeling tremendously guilty. "I *do* love Love Ape—it's just that I need more."

"Love Ape *have* more," he said.

Now I was really concerned. My Love Ape was witty *and* smart.

"OK, Love Ape, you win. I admit it, I have a man who has it all—curiosity, intelligence, looks, money, and refined primitive skills. I am truly blessed, thank God Almighty. There, are you happy?"

"Love Ape happy," he said triumphantly. "Love Ape *real* happy."

I wonder, what do monkeys do in the spring?

## Cats

My cat annoys me more than ever. This morning I woke up and she was sitting at the kitchen table, holding a sign that said "I'm worth every penny and don't you forget it." I could have bought a lot with that five-dollar pet tax money—five chocolate cake mixes, eighteen bars of Irish Spring, or a new toothbrush. I can tell my cat thinks it's funny.

"You shouldn't project human characteristics onto Nimrod," says my husband. "Cats aren't that smart."

"You're wrong," I say. "I'll bet you five dollars both of our cats sit at the kitchen table and smoke cigars as soon as we leave for work. You underestimate the dynamics of the feline underworld."

"Well, the button's always been a little loose, but now it's hanging by a faded thread," he said. "There is no such thing as a feline underworld."

"Believe what you wish," I say, "but it's no coincidence that Nimrod pollutes by your side of the bed when you buy Alley Cat instead of Little Friskies. Next thing you know there'll be a whole new line of cat products by L'Oreal, and Nimrod will be wearing a T-shirt that says, ' Because I'm worth it.'"

"Gary's a pretty good cat," says my husband. "I don't mind forking out five bucks for him. He's really more like a dog than a cat, anyway."

"Gary tries on your hats as soon as you're out of the driveway," I say. "He stretches out on your side of the bed and flicks the remote incessantly."

My husband looks at me with a moment-of-truth stare, and I know what he's thinking: Most of the women in your family lived to be over a hundred, and so will you.

"Would you like to go to the dump with me?" he asks.

"No," I say. "I've given up any hope of ever seeing a rat there—that place is more organized than Betty Crocker's panty drawer."

My husband leaves, and the house is quiet—the kids and the cats are sleeping, and I have time to ponder life for a while. It's easy to feel thankful when everyone's gone or asleep, and I feel thankful for many things.

I feel thankful that we have little more than a pet tax to gripe about, and I feel thankful for a vivid imagination that encompasses the feline underworld. It's good that spring is just around the corner, and I'm grateful for my husband and my children and my cats and an organized dump.

I feel thankful that I did get to see a rat just once in my life—it was at my hometown H.G. Hill grocery store, and a meat department employee chased it out of the store and whacked it with a broom. It was the size of a cat, and since then, I have yearned to see another rat, but I never have.

There's always hope, though, and I'm especially thankful for that.

## My Left Brain

Southern parents are notorious for pegging their children, and I was no exception. Among other things, I was informed from an early age that while I did not appear to have much of a brain at all, it went without question that I had no left brain whatsoever.

For years, I was referred to as a "creative child," whose goal in life was to make the Guinness Book of World Records for writing notes in school and flunking out in math. Being the baby in my family did not help matters any, because my older sisters would gang up against me with my parents in an attempt to create what is known in psychological circles as a self-fulfilling prophecy.

Simply put, this means that we become what we are told we are, to fulfill the expectations and needs of others.

Deep down, I always thought it was a bunch of hogwash. Still, I questioned my own beliefs back when I was in fourth grade, during the "new math" era. My father, a self-proclaimed math expert, would sit down with me at night to help me with my math homework, although I never asked for his assistance. In fact, his presence frustrated me to no end, because the only words he ever uttered were, "In other words."

There we would sit at the chipped green kitchen table with the math book open and my wide-ruled notebook paper waiting with empty lines. My father would then attempt to launch into an in-depth explanation of Base Five, and the only thing he ever said was, "In other words, blah, blah, blah."

I quickly ascertained that he did not know what he was talking about. Finally, in desperation I would scream, "WHAT other words?"

This did not please my father, and he would squirm and accuse me of being a brat. My mother, upon witnessing the potential escalation of the nightly scene, would always say, "Just leave her alone, hon. She's right-brained."

My father would snort and light up a Winston, and I would grab my paper and fly out of the kitchen and do my math all by myself. In other words, I got the job done, but somehow they never noticed.

For reasons too kinked to articulate, my family had a need for me to be "right-brained," and I never gave it much thought. I was just thankful to be able to hold on to the notion that I could get the job done in my own way, whether it be math or music or basketball.

In my life, the path has been crooked, but I have always arrived at my destination intact. Even back then, I recognized this about myself, yet I knew I would never hear it from my family.

For the most part, I have clung to the image I formed of myself at an early age. However, I did buy into the right-brain label, simply because it didn't matter that much to me. Through the years, my perception of a right-brain person indicated a sense of thrill-seeking creativity, an inability to do math, and a probability of never completing a task.

So imagine my surprise when I recently took an online test to determine which side of my brain was dominant, and discovered that I was LEFT-BRAINED! My world was rocked! It was last Saturday morning at five o'clock, and upon learning that I was left-brained, I immediately ran into the bedroom and shook my husband until his own left brain nearly rattled out of his head.

"Guess what!" I screamed. "I'm left-brained, just like you! Do you realize what this means? It means I am logical, linear, sequential, symbolic, verbal, and reality-based!"

He never even opened his eyes, but he did mutter, "I don't believe it."

"You're just like the rest of them," I said. "You want me to be right-brained so that you can accuse me of being fantasy-oriented and illogical. You just wait and see, Lefty. Things are gonna be different now. I always knew I was secretly good at math."

"Well, I guess this means you can do our taxes from now on," he said.

Later that day he left to play golf, and I took five more brain tests, ALL of which indicated that my left brain was dominant.

As with any major life change, this will take some time for me to process. But now that I am logical, linear, and sequential, it will take much less time than it would have taken back in my right-brain days.

Logical, linear, and sequential. Has a certain ring to it, don't you think?

## Hummus

What did we do before hummus? Or perhaps the question is, "Where have I been all my life?" I vaguely recall going to restaurants or parties minus the hummus on the appetizer menu, and my stomach and my husband and I got along just fine.

As anyone with a morsel of culture knows, hummus, or "hummus bi tahini," is a dip or spread made of mashed chickpeas, sesame tahini, lemon juice, and garlic, and it is popular throughout the Middle Eastern world.

Perhaps that could explain why my stomach detonated last night after indulging in the trendy muck.

I was first introduced to hummus two years ago when I was with my daughters at a quaint restaurant in Nashville. We had just been seated, and we were looking at our menus, when one daughter whispered to the other daughter, "They have good hummus." And then they gave each other that knowing look that said, Mom doesn't know what hummus is. She still thinks spinach dip makes her look sophisticated.

My next encounter with hummus was in a restaurant down in St. Petersburg, Florida, just last year. The waiter pranced over to our table and took our drink order, then described the specials and main courses in typical Restaurantese, and then he closed his eyes in a spiritual trance and hummed the words, "Would you like to hear about our hummus?"

"Yeah," my husband said. "What is it?"

The waiter stood still and silent with his eyes closed and whispered, "Our hummus is made of the finest chickpeas in the world, with a hint of sesame tahini imported from Egypt, and just the right blend of lemon juice, garlic, and salt from the Dead Sea."

"We'll take it," my husband said, and when it arrived he ate the whole dish in one bite on a piece of flatbread.

Later that night, his stomach detonated and blew the sheetrock off the walls at two in the morning. A warning to soon-to-be married couples: Do not eat hummus on your wedding night. In fact, you should not eat hummus for at least the first three years of marriage, unless you have a great pre-nup agreement.

My latest and FINAL encounter with hummus occurred just last night at TPAC, otherwise known as Tennessee Performing Arts Center, where my husband and I went with a group to watch Irving Berlin's *White Christmas*.

The third time was no charm, and again there was detonation in the night. Let it be here and forevermore known that I will never eat hummus again, no matter how unsophisticated I appear to be. I will graze in a fresh patch of turnip greens before hummus will ever touch my lips again.

The whole hummus thing led me to research the explosive dish, and I ran across this astounding fact: Hummus Ful is hummus topped with a paste made from one of Hannibal Lector's favorite foods, fava beans.

Kinda makes you wonder what else is in there.

## Be Your Own Vegetable

My old friend Nicole had a case of the blahs, so I took her out to lunch in an attempt to cheer her up. In addition to my Good Samaritan intentions, I looked forward to the spinach dip high.

Nicole had definite cause for concern: She'd recently filed for divorce, was unemployed, and had begun knitting a red toboggan for Clacker, her twenty-year-old parrot.

We were sitting in a private booth at our favorite out-of-town restaurant, and when the spinach dip arrived, I began to inhale. I knew all I had to do was sit and eat, while Nicole spilled her heart, and it worked out perfectly. She needed to talk, and I wanted to eat.

"So how've you been feeling?" I asked.

"Okay, I guess," she said. "Nights and weekends are the worst, especially now that it's cold."

"Nicole, I don't mean to sound judgmental or anything, but *you left him,* after fourteen years of marriage, right when the mutual funds were beginning to sweetly expand, like an accordion in slow motion. Why?"

Nicole leaned toward me and looked at me with eyes so piercing that my tortilla chip froze in mid-air.

"Everything about him began to look like a mushroom," she whispered. "Please, don't say anything about this to anyone—I'm ashamed to admit it, even to myself. But it's true: I could not stand to live out the rest of my days with a withering fungus."

I was stunned. At this stage of the game, most women have mastered the art of convincing themselves their man looks like a nicely weathered Johnny Depp or Brad Pitt.

"A mushroom?" I asked. "And how are you going to explain this to the judge?"

"I'll cross that bridge when I come to it," said Nicole. "Besides, I don't look so hot myself. If I were a vegetable, how would you describe me?"

"I really don't want to answer that question," I said.

"Oh come on," she said. "Where would you find me in your vegetable garden?"

"Okay, you're a snow pea, all young and new and delicate and tender. Now, are you happy?"

"Not really," she said. "I feel like I've been sitting on the edge of the pew in church for twenty years, waiting to get out so I can smoke a cigarette."

"Well, light up, sister—we're in the smoking section. Who's stopping you?"

Again, the piercing stare.

"Would you please stop staring at me?" I said. "You're ruining my spinach dip rush."

"Why didn't you ask me what vegetable I thought you looked like?" Nicole asked.

"Nicole," I said, placing down my chip. "Listen carefully. I used to dream of being a slim pod of okra, or a fresh green corn stalk, blowing gently in the wind. I, too, used to feel like I'd been sitting on the edge of the pew in church for twenty years, waiting to get out so I could smoke a cigarette."

"So what happened?" asked Nicole. "Did you give up the fresh corn stalk dream and light up?"

"No. I realized I already was a fresh corn stalk that would forever blow in the wind, and that no one could take that perception away from me. And I never lit up, although I still want to at times, because doing so would merely deepen the desire."

"So you really don't care if I think you look like a giant zucchini or an overstuffed pumpkin?"

"Not a bit. Worrying about what you think is a waste of my time."

"So how did you figure all this stuff out? Were you a man in a previous life or something? And how do you know what vegetable you are?" she asked.

"You have to figure that out for yourself. Whatever you do, don't ask anyone to do it for you. Remember, you have to be your own vegetable."

Be your own vegetable. Now that's one resolution I can keep.

## What Do You Want on Your Tombstone?

Today's topic is morbid but intriguing: What do you want on your tombstone?

I can think of a number of sentiments.

- "She tried."
- "When I told him to hold the pickle, he just went nuts."
- "Gone to greet Rover in fields of green clover."

I know, I know. Death is not funny. But when it's time for my eternal swim in the Dead Sea, I hope there's still some room for laughter.

When I die, I want my husband and children to be overcome with tremendous guilt, not grief. All the home-cooked meals, the labor pains, chicken pox and colic—all these things have endless guilt potential. My motto is,

Where there's guilt, there's hope. But who am I kidding? Guilt dies with the deceased.

Take a man, for example. He has been married for thirty years. Established name, successful kids, good church home, grows tomatoes in the back yard. His wife has always worked "inside the home" and greets him at the door every evening with a hug and a smile. So what if she's had a few too many Twinkies—she's built her life around him and the children, and of course, Rover.

Then one day a Twinkie gets wedged in her esophagus, and bam! She's gone, just like that. The whole town pays their respects at the funeral home because she was such a wonderful wife, mother, and person. Flowers are all over the place—peace lilies, gardenias, magnolias, mums, daisies, the works.

But how quickly they wilt.

Why? Because there are pie pimps everywhere. Casserole queens, soup sluts, just waiting to make their move and pounce on that hungry man.

Some of these women will wait a week to toss their bait. Others deliver the day after. At this stage of the game, it's simply a matter of "may the best pie win."

Works almost every time, because men are easy. But they are too smart to waste their time trying to figure out why.

Sure, I have issues. I still cry when I listen to "Puff the Magic Dragon," and I never really got past *Charlotte's Web*. I spend time pondering over whether to read *Relationship Rescue* or *How to Write Funny*. It's possible that I am not a normal person, but I derive great pleasure and hours of satisfaction with my skewed and jaded views.

Life is ironic. Even though I detest hypocrisy, I am perhaps the most hypocritical of all. If my husband suffocated on a Twinkie, I might, at some point, be tempted to deliver a pie to a rich old codger. Lately, though, I've been thinking it would be best to take him out to eat at that Mexican restaurant in Hohenwald.

There was a time when my husband and I cried at the thought of each others' Twinkie demise. Now our love is stronger than ever, and I would still cry, especially if it had been a long slow choke. But I am older now, and more realistic. I know how much he likes pie. I know how horrible it would be to get cold and scared in the night. And I owe these realizations all to him and to the good times he has brought me.

But he'd better wait at least a year, or he'll be sorry.

## Bacon Wars

We reach a point in life where eating becomes a hobby. Lucky for us, we live in an area of the country where new restaurants sprout from the earth as if the land has taken fertility drugs. Even if it is a chain restaurant that we have been going to for years in another location, we get excited because we haven't been to the new one yet.

So my husband and I recently traveled north to the new restaurant that is cozy and nostalgic and has an old country store inside. It had only been open for two weeks, so it was definitely new. There were people waiting on us every thirty seconds to warm up our coffee or bring us more biscuits. He ordered the Grandpappy Sampler, and I ordered the Granny Platter, and between the two of us, we wiped out one of the five remaining farms left in the county.

The new waitress, ever eager to please, took our order and wrote down everything my husband wanted, and then she poofed into the kitchen. Meanwhile, a young male appeared, saying that he would now be taking care of our food. Suddenly, the waitress was standing beside him, and right before our eyes they got into an argument over my husband's bacon.

"Sir, have you got your bacon?" he said, sweat beading up on his forehead. "I'll get it for you, sir, because I'm taking care of you now. Your bacon will be here any minute."

The young waitress staked her claim and stepped forward. "I'm taking care of the bacon," she said, giving him the bacon glare of the century. "This is my table." And then they both poofed into the kitchen.

"Isn't this great?" I said to my husband. "We've never had anybody fight over us before. I just love it!"

"You would," he said. "Just calm down. This is a new restaurant, and they're still getting the kinks worked out."

"Well, you can be mature if you want to," I said, "but I am going to enjoy this once-in-a-lifetime opportunity. I'll probably get a free pork chop out of this one."

The young waiter reappeared, his entire head glazed with sweat. It was evident that a matter of epidemic proportions had encompassed his being.

"Sir, have you got your bacon yet?" he asked. "I'm sorry about the mix-up, Sir. She just doesn't know what she's doing. You can complain to management, Sir. I will get yo u that bacon if it's the last thing I do."

"Don't worry about it," said my husband. "Everything is fine."

The waiter slumped his shoulders and said, "I've been working here for two weeks, and it feels like two years. I need a vacation."

A nerve was hit, deep within the core of my soul. At this point I realized this young man's greatest desire did not involve the perfection of my food or its service. But he didn't notice, because he was in full whine mode, unaware that there were no violins playing.

Long after he'd worn out his welcome, he sat down beside my husband and said, "Man, I feel really bad about that bacon. I'm going to get it for you, I promise." Suddenly, the kid was our newly adopted son. He looked at me with his hair hanging down over his eyes and said, "You know, I've noticed that when people start to get full, they begin to eat real slow."

I leaned over and gave him a bacon glare. "Yeah, it kind of works that way," I said.

My husband gave me a killer look, and our new son stood up and stretched and yawned. "Well, I guess I'd better get back there and check on your bacon, Sir. It'll be out here any minute."

As soon as he disappeared, the young waitress popped out from behind a plow. "Sir, I brought you some bacon. And I'm sorry he took over my table. I'll take care of everything, Sir."

With absolute predictability, our new son appeared. "Where did you get that bacon?" he cried. "This is not fair! I have been working here for two whole weeks, and this is my table. Sir, I'm going to get management right now."

"Don't worry about it," said my husband. "We've had plenty to eat, and everything was fine. Goodbye."

On our way to the car I noticed the new clone restaurant next door, with a packed parking lot, but somehow the thrill was gone. A full stomach will do that to a person.

## Diet Book

In this struggling economy, it helps to throw away that scarcity mentality and seek out the weaknesses in people. It has been a lifelong vague dream of mine to write a diet book, but deep down I always knew this would entail change in my diet and exercise routine, so I placed the endeavor on the back burner and simmered it with the rest of my past.

The dream was stirred about two months ago, when I stumbled upon some high-tech scales that claimed to not only digitally announce your weight, but also your BMI and your bone density. And so I bought the contraption, and as I always do with any new appliance, I let it sit in the house for a month or two, occasionally glancing at it before I actually plug it in, turn it on, or step on it.

One morning just out of the blue, I stepped onto the scales in much the same way as I stepped onto the high dive and dove into the water without looking down, back in June 1968. Let's just say the water still stings.

Let's just say it's okay to hiss and scream at appliances and call them all sorts of names. Let's just say these suckers do not lie. No matter how much you hold your breath or hang on to the bathroom sink or stand on one foot or keep one eye closed, the number stays the same.

As they say, the truth will make you lie. Until you have some sort of awakening, that is. Something like a good look in the mirror with your contacts in after the steam from the shower has left the room. Or perhaps a co-worker who has put on a pound or two through the years, then suddenly melts down to the size of a Hershey's Kiss right before your eyes in a seemingly effortless manner.

Such was the case with me. While I watched my co-worker melt, she gave me the perfect title for my diet book: *Poof!* The next step was to find out her secret, so I asked her, and she told me. Essentially, I would have to eat dandelions and drink green tea for two weeks, but after that I could have some fruit, and so I plunged into my new commitment like a new young bride in the month of June.

And now I have a better title for my diet book: *I Went on a Diet and My Husband Lost Twenty Pounds*. Folks, it is true.

On the third day of my diet, my husband stepped down from the scales and said, "Are those scales right? I've lost ten pounds!"

Was I supposed to be HAPPY about this? Yes, I was. And so I said, "That's great, honey munchkin. Pretty soon you'll be right up there with me!"

The next week he proclaimed, "I have lost ten more pounds!"

"Isn't life grand?" I said to him with a smile on my face and a carrot stick in my heart.

Back at the job, my co-worker was flouncing around in her brand new teeny-tiny clothes, and she looked happy, like my husband. Which gave me yet another title for my diet book: *I Liked You Better When You Were Fat*.

Not that either of them was ever fat, and they certainly aren't now! Their success just happened to lend itself to a spiffy new title.

Meanwhile, I'm getting my courage up. In a little while I'm going to tiptoe down the hall, gently turn on the bathroom light, hold on to the side of the sink, hold my breath with one eye shut, and face the music.

## Smoking

My mother was born with a cigarette hanging out of her mouth. This set the stage for embryonic tendencies embedded within me, and it also allowed me to blame my mother for numerous quirks of my own that manifest themselves unto this day.

Although my mother never stopped smoking, and it was probably a factor in her death, she did express remorse from time to time. She even apologized, which was a rarity for her. "I'm sorry, hon," she'd say, "but my hemorrhoids nearly killed me when I was pregnant with you. L&M's were the only thing that helped . . . I'll bet you craved them when you were a little fetus."

I started smoking when I was a teenager, but quit after I got married and became pregnant, in spite of the hemorrhoids. But I forgave my mother because they didn't know about the harmful effects of smoking back then. Everyone on *I Love Lucy* smoked, and it was somewhat of a norm, especially among men.

I have a picture of my mother when she was pregnant with me, standing beside my uncle and my two older sisters. It must have been a stressful time, because at full-term, my mother looked like a toothpick that had swallowed a green pea. At birth, I only weighed six pounds, but in no time I turned out to be a right hefty gal.

Everyone in my entire family smoked, especially after church. After all, smoking tends to relieve stress and allow people to temporarily kick back into their true selves. Our church experience, on the other hand, did just the opposite. Damnation, condemnation, and pontification are major causes of smoking.

After church, it was somehow acceptable for men to stand out on the sidewalk and smoke, but heaven forbid if a woman should light up. After we stood around and chatted with the brethren and sistren, my sisters and I would climb into the back seat of my parents' car for the ride home, which was just down the street. My father would light up another one, and my mother would lie down in the front seat and rasp, "Hon, gimme a drag of that."

My sisters and I would stare at the desperate clench of our mother's hand, and then we would stare at each other through the haze of smoke.

I once went out with a man who had raised bees for so long that he himself had begun to resemble a bee. He picked me up and drove me to the next town for dinner, and I lit up about half a mile down the road.

"I didn't know you smoked," he said. "If I'd known that, I never would have asked you out!"

"If I'd known you cared, I never would have gone," I replied.

Surprisingly, he asked me out again, but I said no.

Smoking fills the hole in the soul, and that's why it's hard to quit. Given time, the hole repairs itself, and life looks better minus the smokescreen.

After all, time is all we have.

## Lobsters in Cyberspace

Cyberspace imitates life. We have the cloned gazillionaire from Brazil who informs us that we have won the lottery if only we will provide essential information, such as bank account numbers, addresses, and home phone numbers.

These people are distant cousins of the door-to-door vacuum cleaner salesman.

Now that I think about it, I haven't seen a door-to-door vacuum cleaner salesman in a long while. Perhaps they have moved upward and outward into Cyberspace, where numerous opportunities await, while their prey sits at the click of the mouse in an attempt to escape the real world.

Another disappointment in Cyberspace is the forwarded e-mail that contains "the unexpected calamity of the day prediction." We have the picture of the woman whose right ear was blown off her head, while talking on her cell phone on her way to a lingerie party. Hovered in a corner, sucking his thumb in a fetal position, we have the ninety-pound man who ate Spam Soufflé after heating it up in the microwave with plastic wrap on top.

The other night I grew weary of such mindless tales of woe, and I entered Television Land on the couch with my husband, where horrific events were taking place by the nanosecond. The oceans were boiling, Yellowstone National Park had erupted and liquefied into a molten stew, and dinosaurs were running amok. Perhaps the most disturbing aspect was that cockroaches had taken over Buckingham Palace, some of them headless, but still running around in search of a jeweled crown and a pomegranate.

"What is this?" I asked.

"This is what will happen after the human race dies out, and the animals take over the world."

"Don't we have enough to worry about in the here and now?" I asked. "Do we have plenty of peanut butter and crackers? And have you checked the fried okra supply lately?"

"Why don't you go watch *True Blood*?" he asked. "You went to sleep last night before Bill bit Sookie, and you will not be disappointed."

So off I trotted to the bedroom to watch my favorite TV show, *True Blood*, truly the best show in the history of the world. I shamelessly admit that I am so hooked on this show that *Dexter* is fading on the horizon. I watched Bill bite Sookie with sweet vampire passion, and I drifted off to sleep and woke up at four a.m. and returned to cyberspace, where the calamity of the day was waiting silently for me.

On that day I had received an e-mail from a friend—a video of Anne Murray singing "How Great Thou Art," and while listening to Anne sing, I simultaneously read about the man in San Diego who stuffed six live lobsters down his pants. The contrast of the hymn mixed with the lobster tale had seriously intrigued me, and just when I got to the good part, my husband stumbled into the room.

"You havin' church in here?" he asked. "Turn that thing down!"

And so I did, without a word, and he quietly went back to bed, and I went back to my calamity. Turns out the lobsters were the kind without pincers, so other than the man getting arrested and having his picture plastered on the walls of Cyberspace, he was unharmed. Whew.

Life is full of close calls—some of them real, some of them imagined, and many of them completely fabricated by the limitless opportunities of Hollywood and Cyberspace.

## Waxing Gibbous

Thanks to an e-mail that I recently received, my life now makes perfect sense. Specifically, the e-mail linked me to a website called On the Day You Were Born, or in other words, The Ultimate Case of Too Much Information.

I now know that at the moment of my conception, which occurred on or about November 5, my parents were either listening to "The Purple People Eater" by Sheb Wooley, or "Don't" by Elvis Presley.

Thanks to On the Day You Were Born, I know every single detail about my life thus far. I know how old I am in dog years; how many BTUs the candles on my next birthday cake will produce; and the number of hours, minutes, and seconds I have lived.

I have learned about my life path compatibility and that my life path number is 5. I am least compatible with those whose life path numbers are 2, 4, 6, 11 and 22. In other words, my husband and children, every single one of them. Furthermore, I have learned that my husband's life path number is compatible with all of our children's life path numbers, and that is why they have always ganged up against me.

After studying the On the Day You Were Born stats for my husband and children, I became convinced that my parents were indeed listening to "Don't" by Elvis Presley at the moment of my conception. Now I understand the source of the original opposition and resistance that has tainted my life.

There is nothing I can do. My life path number is 5, and that's that. The good news is, I now have proof that my husband is, well, stubborn. Here is what his life path number says about him: *You have the kind of will power that is often mistaken for sheer stubbornness.*

On the day my husband was born, the moon's phase was full, and on the day I was born the moon was waxing gibbous. I don't know what that means but it sounds gooey to me. I would have preferred a new moon or a crescent moon, but waxing gibbous is what I got. At the moment of my conception, somewhere near the end of "Don't" by Elvis Presley, my mother probably looked out the window and said, "Gad, the moon is waxing gibbous."

"Gad" was my mother's favorite word, and she said it whenever she became alarmed, which was approximately every three seconds. My sisters and I always wondered what "gad" meant. My mother also used other words and expressions too numerous to mention, but one of them was "ookie doo," which somehow reminds me of "waxing gibbous."

Some information is best left unknown, such as the details of the moment of our conception. The past is the past and all we can do is march forward with our incompatible life numbers. Still, I can't help but wonder how it might have been if the moon had been full and my parents had been listening to "Volare" by Domenico Modugno.

I'll never know, and that's a very good thing.

## Bedtime Conversations

There is something comforting about bedtime conversations. You're lying there at the end of the day while your family is nodding off, listening to the quiet conversation. There's just something about it.

As a child I used to like to listen to my parents talk right before they went to sleep. I never heard what they said—I just knew they sounded relieved that they had survived the day and that they were about to embark on precious slumber, and maybe even a good dream filled with lollipops and cotton candy. At least that was my interpretation.

As an adult, I have come to appreciate those last words spoken before drifting off into dreamland, or nightmareland, whatever the case may be.

Our four children are all grown up now for the most part, even though the two sons are still in college. The older son tells me he has moved his graduation date into the new millennium and that's okay because it is not true: His graduation date is scheduled December 2012, and we are proud of him and we look forward to knocking another one off the family payroll. However, we will keep him on the family cell phone plan until he lands a job.

The younger son proclaims he is a junior in college, and I will take his word on that because it is fun to believe his proclamation is possibly true. If it is not true, I will cross that bridge when I come to it. Worse things have happened indeed.

When our two sons were young, they shared a bedroom with bunk beds and I used to love to hear them talk before drifting off to sleep. The thing was, only one of them talked, and it was Gus, the baby, who is much like me in that realm. Patrick, the older son, has never been much of a talker, and he is much like my husband in that realm.

Most nights, the conversation would go like this: Gus would be yakking about school and soccer and his teachers and anything that popped into his little head, and Patrick, the quiet one, would say, "Gus, don't you ever shut up? Just shut up and go to sleep!"

And then there would be silence.

But one night there was not silence, because they got into an argument over who was better: God or Jesus. At the time, they were enrolled in a "mother's day out" program, which was located inside a local church where it was legal to speak of God and Jesus. I will add that this was one of the best "mother's day out" programs in town, and I will always be thankful for the experiences my children had there.

On the night as I lay in my bed listening to their conversation about God versus Jesus, an unusual tension began to rise from their bedroom.

Patrick, the quiet and older son, took God's side, and Gus took Jesus's side, and serious competition set in. Patrick had proof that God was better and Gus had proof that Jesus reigned, and the result was yelling and tears and gnashing of baby teeth.

I went in there and asked, "What in the world are you two arguing about? Just go to sleep!"

Gus cried, "Patrick said God was better than Jesus and that's not true! Jesus is better than God!"

Patrick, the quiet and older son said, "He doesn't know what he's talking about—he's just a kid. Everyone knows that God is better than Jesus."

I assured them both God and Jesus were good, and competition was also good, but in this case it was unnecessary to argue or compete. And then I said, "Just be quiet and go to sleep," and they did.

To my knowledge, they never argued about God and Jesus again, but the memory will always remain in a sweet place in my heart, right next to the place in my heart that will experience glee when they receive their college diplomas and land their own jobs.

In the meantime, I believe God and Jesus are looking over both of them, along with the rest of us.

That is my hope and my prayer and my final thought before drifting off to sleep, and it shall forever be.

## Cleaning My Daughter's House

There is nothing on earth as powerful as maternal instinct. When Cain killed Abel, Eve probably killed Cain—they just left that part out of the Bible, or like so many details throughout history, it was lost in translation. Perhaps the slant was not right for the intent of the writers.

Biblical opinions aside, I digress, but only for a moment. If Eve did not clobber Cain with a fig tree, and not a fig branch, I guarantee you she did something to him, for she was also the mother of Abel, the slain. Cain did a bad, bad thing there, and mothers do not take lightly to harmful acts inflicted upon their children.

\* \* \*

Today I am cleaning my daughter's house. It is more fun to clean another woman's house than my own, but still this is a challenge, especially for me, a woman who is not even distantly related to Betty Crocker, who as we all know was a fictitious character. In truth, Betty Crocker did not exist, and if she did, today she would be a cringe-woman because of her prudish ways—her goal in life was to bake the perfect cookie—and in today's world many women do not get a chance to bake the perfect cookie because they work "outside the home," like my daughter does. If young mothers ever get a chance to plop down and eat a cookie at the end of a long day, it is store-bought and grabbed and swallowed whole by the wild banshee toddler at hand.

This is the truth. There is nothing lost in translation here, and parents, whether single or not, know it.

Sometimes in life, when we order the prescription for our children that we desire and envision for ourselves, the prescription has either run out or the kid won't swallow the pill. Such is the case with my daughter, whom I dearly love, regardless of the choices she has made in her life.

After all, it is her life, not my life, and after fifty-three years, I accept that.

Before I recently retired from teaching school since 1981, with a degree and much experience in teaching various realms of special education, I saw clearly and firsthand the children who did not fulfill the dream of the parent or swallow the pill of the prescription. I saw the broken hearts of parents who knew their daughters or sons would never have a baby, much less a house of their own to clean, and my career changed my perception of parenthood.

No, we do not always get what we want, and the Lord does indeed work in mysterious ways. Still, there is that original hope and perception—that unfulfilled dream that will never come to fruition, because we are what we are, take it or leave it. With children, we take what we get, and mothers rarely leave it. Luckily, there are many fathers who stand by and face the music, as well.

So I am cleaning my daughter's house today, but it is more than a tangible thing. I am playing the role of the mother I always wanted, and that is OK as long as I know when to stop, for we each have our own lives, and we were all meant to embrace our own joy, regardless of the heartaches of motherhood and life.

There are broken crayons on my daughter's floor and purple crayon paintings etched on the wall, and neon pink Play-Doh adorns the floor, compliments of her toddler, and my perfect grandbaby Lily. There are scattered bills, coupons, receipts and torn curtains. And this is only the beginning.

But I have to ask myself, "What did I expect?" After all, it's not as if I were the model child. I was energetic and wild and full of creative ideas, much to my mother's dismay. My mother is dead, and I have not changed.

My daughter is a successful accountant—driven as a bull—a number cruncher who works harder than anyone I have ever known.

I am proud of her, and I am proud that she has been able to buy a house for me to clean, and to have a toddler who knows how to get the most out of a can of Play-Doh. And while my daughter did not fill my prescription, I no longer care.

I only wish every child could grow up and buy a house to clean, and perhaps have a toddler to chase down.

I often think of the forgotten children and their parents, because in my previous career, I worked with them for so long, and I caught a unique glimpse into their families and the heartaches therein, the heartaches that most people never see or even think about. After all, if it doesn't happen to us, it doesn't happen, period.

And while my heart aches with disappointment from time to time, as do all parents' hearts, I know that I am one of the lucky ones, and for that I am most thankful.

## Lily

*Consider the lilies of the field, how they grow: they neither toil nor spin; and yet I say to you that even Solomon in all his glory was not arrayed like one of these.*

—Matthew 6:28-29

When I was a child I attended my church regularly, just like it instructed me to do on the back of the Purity milk carton. In church, I memorized the Beatitudes, and I often heard them cited from the pulpit. Sometimes I heard them maimed and twisted and gnarled and spewed from the pulpit, but there was one part of the Sermon on the Mount that even the most skewed perceptions and selfish agendas could not tarnish: Consider the lilies.

I always loved the words "Consider the lilies" and the way they resonated in my heart. Here at the end of 2009, those words have special and everlasting meaning to me because the year delivered unto me a new granddaughter named Lily.

Life is funny. Just when you begin to think you have your children figured out, along comes a grandbaby, and everything changes. For the better, I might add. Oh, I'm not the first to become a grandparent, and I certainly won't be the last, so I won't delve into the land of self-indulgence here, although it is tempting. That's merely one aspect of being a grandparent: You don't really care how bored your friends are when you show them the five million pictures of your grandbaby. My mother used to say, "Every old crow thinks hers is the blackest," and she was right.

What you do care about is the very best for your grandbaby. By this stage of the game, you have learned from the mistakes you made with your own children, and you want your grandchild to become the beneficiary of your experience. So here at the end of 2009, I want to pass along a few words of wisdom to Lily, just in case she might benefit from them some day.

I want Lily to know that she should never allow her rock-bottom-moments to become her defining moments, although people may attempt to do this to her. She alone has the capacity to learn to define herself and to forget about the lives other people may prescribe for her, in spite of her rock-bottom moments. And another thing . . . we all have rock-bottom moments, some of them more obvious than others, but painful nevertheless.

I want her to know that some of us find our religion and some of us lose our religion, but God still loves us anyway. She should know that in writing and in life, what we leave out is more important than what we put in.

I hope Lily learns to be her own best friend, for the world would be a safe, happy, and peaceful place if we all learned that simple lesson. I want her to know that shame, while sometimes necessary, is an overrated emotion. God did not intend for us to drown in the swamp of shame throughout our lives.

There are so many things I want Lily to know, and hopefully, she will learn even more than I have along the way. Life is fleeting, and it is a gift that sometimes presents itself in poetic form: *Sunday knocked at my door, Wednesday answered, and Saturday said goodbye.*

Enjoy every possible moment while you can, and know that you were loved.

# MEMORY BOULEVARD

## The Zipper

It's fair week in my old hometown, the week when the weather always changed to a cool crisp and you dug around in the winter clothes for your favorite sweater. From my upstairs bedroom window, I could see the double Ferris wheel and hear the screams of people on rides who paid to get flipped and flown through the air. But most of the time I was not looking out my window because I was there every night, circling the midway with my friends and consuming massive amounts of greasy corn dogs and snow cones and cotton candy and Lion's Club hamburgers and homemade pies.

There is a certain mystique that forever etches the carnival experience into our hearts, for the midway arena is filled with adventures of love and fear and excitement and hunger of all sorts. As a young child, I can recall sitting at the top of the double Ferris wheel with my father, listening to Petula Clark singing "Downtown," while I looked down on the crowd. And as an eighth grader, I can recall sitting at the top of the double Ferris wheel with a SOPHOMORE whom I had admired for years, and when he slipped his arm around me, I lost the capacity to hear music or feel anything other than sheer exhilaration. I was close to heaven up there, wearing one of those cotton peasant shirts with a little bow in the middle, a Creamsicle orange as I recall, and on that night at the top of the double Ferris wheel, I reached the pinnacle of life. Somehow, he failed to notice this and never even called, but such is the life of the carnival ride.

My fair experiences vacillated between heart-fluttering moments at the top of the double Ferris wheel and gut-wrenching jolts on the Zipper with my two best friends. The Zipper was our favorite ride and the three of us loved to squeeze in there and make it flip over and over and over, while we screamed our lungs out. One fateful night we stuffed ourselves into the cage of the Zipper and conned the operator into a free ride, a double-your-pleasure experience. Earlier, we had eaten my mother's lasagna, two large pizzas, Lion's Club hamburgers, and corn dogs fried in the original grease from the beginning of time.

It was an exceptional Zipper cage—a record-setting flipper, and toward the end of the first ride my friend to the right said, "Uh oh. I'm going to throw up." The first ride ended, and we begged the Zipper man to let us off, but he grinned and said, "No, no, no . . . free ride!"

And so at the start of the free ride, the cage began to flip again, and the fluid began to fly. My nauseous friend had on a white sweatshirt, and my friend to the left had a tendency to laugh hysterically and wet her pants whenever anything horrible happened. With each flip the cage became wilder and wetter and I was stuck in the middle of my two best friends. Whenever we would pass him at the bottom, I would scream to the Zipper operator, "Please let us off—please, please, please, let us off!"

But he just grinned and screamed, "Free ride, baby! Free ride!"

Ah, those were the days when tattoos were rare, and most of the people who had them traveled with the fair. I always wondered about the makings of those ride operators, but it was one of those things that was easy to overlook, like smoking causes lung cancer and gossip is malicious.

The ride ended and my hysterical laughing friend's father picked us up, along with one of his male friends. Meanwhile, my nauseous friend's white shirt was stained with a big orange glob and she was mortified because among other things, she was a contender for the Fairest of the Fair pageant that year.

We made it to the car and climbed in, and the father's friend sniffed around and rolled down the window. "You smell something?" he asked.

"Yeah," said the father. "I sure do." These were prominent men, honorable and dignified, and we had clearly brought them to their knees.

Whoever said, "Ain't no such thing as a free ride" was right. But still my quest continues, in search of the top of a double Ferris wheel and a giant corn dog that could make a hog barf, for such is the life of the carnival ride.

## Those Were the Days

Maybe it's the hot, lazy days of summer, or maybe it was seeing Fred Thompson on *The Daily Show with Jon Stewart* talking about our hometown of Lawrenceburg, Tennessee, that's caused me to be nostalgic these past few days.

Just yesterday my husband said, "Er . . . have you noticed the new dryer down in the basement? Do you think it WORKS? And what about our new plan to take our entire house to Goodwill? Are you going to work on that today? Are you? Are you?"

I was spread out like a melted Hershey bar on our leather couch, smack dab in front of the fan that would turn into a helicopter if only it had a propeller on top. "I'm thinking about my hometown," I said. "The town square. Just run along now." And then I stood upside down in front of the fan and turned it up full blast and felt the cool air from heaven flow down the back of my neck, and it made me smile. It doesn't take much these days.

There's just something about a town square that takes us back to the day when small towns would close for business on certain days of the week, and in my town that day was Thursday. There were so many appealing stores on our town square that it was unnecessary to pick a favorite, because each store had its place for each phase of our lives. I will say that I did not have a fondness for the children's Parks Belk, because when my mother took me there to buy a training bra, the sales clerk said I was already trained.

During the fourth- and fifth-grade years, that sweet pre-pubescent time of life, my friends and I liked to go to Lay's dime store to look at school supplies. I can still recall the pink and yellow cloth-covered notebook, plastered with huge '70s flowers that I bought one year. Turned out everyone else had bought the same one, but such is life in a small-town world.

Over at Holland's Drug Store, we loved to sample the Yardley Pot o' Gloss behind the glass counter, and we would get ice cream cones there after church on Wednesday night. I can remember thinking, "Better enjoy this cold stuff before you get to the Bad Place," and somehow the double-dip strawberry cone would melt away all my worries of fire and brimstone and grinning devils.

The upstairs of Kuhn's was otherwise known as "where the toys were," and the mere act of walking up the old wooden steps to see the toys was almost as exciting as Christmas morning. Perhaps it was the new stuff in an old place, or maybe it was just the innocence of childhood—I don't know. I just know that while my mother was over at the main Parks Belk, probably buying big-girl bras, I was checking out the Little Kiddles upstairs at Kuhn's.

On Sunday afternoons I would go to Crockett Theatre with a church-friend to watch a double feature. This was back before anybody paid much attention to the rating of a movie, and my favorite movie memory is the day we watched *The Getaway* and *Bonnie and Clyde*, all in one day on a Sunday afternoon when I was in the sixth grade.

To this day, I am in awe of Steve McQueen and the chase scene in *The Getaway*, and Faye Dunaway and Warren Beatty left a bullet-ridden impression, as well.

Over at Irwin's, the draw was the glass case of warm cashews. During my senior year, when a friend and I took a third-period break from school due to a severe case of senior slump, we just happened to run into my grandfather who was standing in front of the store. "What are you two doing down here?" he asked.

"We're just buying some nuts," I said, and the three of us laughed and went on our merry ways. The topic was never brought up in my family, and that is one of the many things I appreciate about my grandfather.

Those were the days, oh yes, those were the days.

## My Hometown

I rarely visit my old hometown, but circumstances bring me down here, and it is a sweet encounter.

I am with my husband, and we drive by my grandparents' farm on the edge of town where the huge maple tree has been replaced by a furniture store, and I hiss and growl like a cat, clawing at the man who built this monstrosity where the old white farmhouse used to sit.

"Stop it with the hex stuff," my husband says. "Your grandfather would be proud of how much money the farm brought—he would like knowing he was able to benefit his family in such a lucrative way, and you know it."

Yes, I know it. Still, I am comforted by the thought that the old pond sits back in the woods—they didn't tear that away—and the thought that maybe the bullfrogs are still out there croaking at night, comforting some small child to sleep while her grandparents rest soundly in the next room.

On down the road, we pass the hardest part: It is the house I grew up in—the one in the middle of town with the big front porch and the old white swing and the big white columns and my mother's flowerboxes. It is impossible for me to look at this porch without seeing my mother stooped over her flowerboxes, pinching petunias.

Now, a doctor owns the house, and the flowerboxes sit empty. He has turned it into a business, and I wonder just what it is that he does in our house, and I think how excited my mother would be at the thought of pap smears being performed in her kitchen.

Out front stands the huge dogwood that we used to hide in and scream at people as they passed by. Once, my sister made me climb up in it and fall out just as the lifeguard from the pool up the street drove by, hoping that he would stop and tend to my broken limbs. She knew exactly when he would drive by, and I fell out of the tree right on cue, but he did not stop. Such is the story of my life—the prince comes galloping to the rescue, but takes one look at me and revs up the old white horse.

We get to the town square, and I see my old friend's sister. It's been twenty-five years, but she knows me and hugs me, and this is good.

My husband is busy, so I wander down the sidewalk and stare into the window of the shoe store that's been there since 1925. Suddenly, I'm back in fourth grade with my best friends, picking out our new school shoes in September—penny loafers? Bee-bops? Around the corner stands the old Lay's five and dime and again I'm taken back. There's that pink-and-yellow-flowered notebook from 1969—the one every girl in my class had at the start of the new school year.

And now I wander into the old corner drugstore, the one that still serves old-fashioned fountain drinks and the best vanilla shakes in the world. Walk in, and you'll see big bottles of Watkins vanilla flavoring and a teenage girl in an apron behind the counter and old men sitting at a table in the back.

I see a man I'd gone to church with, the old elder's son. "Do you remember me?" I ask.

"Why sure I remember you," he says, shaking my hand and smiling at me. "Why wouldn't I?"

My husband and I go to a restaurant, and a classmate walks by with his wife. He sticks out his hand and tells me his name without necessity. He was a senior when I was a sophomore, and one does not forget such things. His mother is also with him, and a memory hits me: It is a slow hot day in July, and a friend and I have just finished grazing in her mama's kitchen—fried chicken, mashed potatoes, fresh green beans, fried corn, cornbread, plus other items too numerous to mention. After lunch we become bored and decide to go out in the middle of the day and decorate various vehicles with shaving cream, our latest favorite pastime. We go over to this senior's house where his car sits out front and we squirt it with that cheap shaving cream in the red-and-white-striped can from Fred's—four for a dollar. We circle his car, running and giggling until the cans are empty, then speed away happy. We go back to her house for dessert and the phone rings. It is the senior's mother. "You girls did a beautiful job. Now get back over here and clean it up."

And so we do, and afterward we laugh long and hard and plan to do any future decorating at night.

Here, in my old hometown, paradise has been paved by parking lots, but people still know my name, and I am the luckiest of girls.

## Grapevines

I wonder if the grape vines are still there.

Lately I've been thinking about the back yard of my childhood home. So long ago, yet still so vivid in my memory, that back yard with the six grape vines in a row close to the property line, and a lone vine of grapes to the side.

There is a picture of my oldest sister standing beside the lone vine of grapes, and like any good picture, it captured a moment. This one would be captioned "caught with her hand in the grape vine jar." The look in her eyes is one of slight embarrassment because her mouth is full of grapes. Either that or she secretly went out and chewed tobacco behind the grape cluster. I'm pretty sure it was a mouthful of grapes that she held in her mouth, and the picture became a family favorite because of the expression on my sister's face and the symbolic nostalgia of the grapevines. She was wearing a pair of shorts and a sleeveless top, and everything about the photograph portrayed the innocence of childhood and the days of summer.

My mother loved those grapevines that produced clusters of juicy Concord grapes late in the summer. While many mothers were browsing through cookbooks or feather dusting the windowsills, my mother was saying, "Hon, the grapes are about ready!" And then she would rub her hands together real fast like a kid at Christmas. It's a wonder they didn't catch on fire with all that friction over the grape excitement.

The grapes were special indeed. In my mind, I view the back yard as a photograph that was framed within the parameters of the grapevines. And even though the frame was a purple beauty, the back yard itself was the true picture.

I learned to ride a bicycle in that back yard, not out of desire, but of necessity, when my Uncle Milas poofed in out of the blue as he often did, and pushed me from behind like I have never been pushed, but it was a good thing. It was a good thing because I was effortlessly riding the little green bicycle from nearby Murray, Ohio, the manufacturing plant, and it felt like I was actually riding on my own. As I began to slow down, I realized I needed to pedal, and then I noticed I was going on my own, and it felt good.

How is it that once you learn to ride a bicycle, you never forget? How is it that once you learn how to swim, you always remember? Your life is permanently altered with each lesson learned. Thank you, Uncle Milas.

My sisters and my friends and I used to lay out in the sun beside the grapevines in the back yard, and of course there was the occasional camping out in the tent that produced good memories, as well.

But there is just something about those grapevines. Right now I can see my oldest sister stretched out in the sun in the back yard beside the grapevines, reading a *Redbook* magazine while my mother is in the house watching *As the World Turns* with our toy poodle Tinkerbell at her side, set to snarl and mangle any possible intruders.

Yes, I wonder if the grapevines are still there. I like to think that they are, but I don't want to know for sure.

## The Student

When I was in third grade, there was a boy in my class who had epileptic seizures, or fits, as they were called back then. I had never heard of an epileptic fit until I witnessed one firsthand. This was back in 1966, and times were different. Every day our teacher would read a verse from the Bible, which sat on her desk at the upper right, diametrically opposed to the wooden paddle that resided on the upper left. Bible, paddle; Bible, paddle; Bible, paddle, then one day it was Bible, paddle, epileptic fit. I had never seen anything like it in my life.

The boy always sat beside the teacher, facing the class, but I never questioned his seating arrangement because my mind was not bent in this manner. I thought about lunch, recess, and going home and getting a 7-Up and some Tom's peanuts from my grandfather's service station, which was next door to our house.

But on the day of the first epileptic fit, after the teacher had read the Bible verse and our coats were hung or thrown back into the cloak room and the paddle was yet unused, the boy began to jerk as if he had stuck a wet finger into an electrical outlet. His eyes rolled back in his head, and his body convulsed as we all watched, while the teacher, an attractive petite woman, would get up and physically restrain him until the convulsions stopped. And then we would go on about our business and the boy would remain in his chair. There was no calling of the principal, no 911, no medication, no panic, just a sense of expected normalcy in an abnormal setting.

The day would progress and we would have the usual reading and social studies, then milk break and recess. Out on the playground, the student would return to his normal state which involved turning his eyelids inside-out and holding his arms out like Frankenstein and coming after us with a grin on his face. This Freddy Kruegeresque behavior scared me, and I have never gotten the image of the inside-out eyelids and the wide-spread grin out of my head. It is only now, in looking back, that I realize the student made the best of a bad situation. He did not seem to be marred by the status of epilepsy; indeed it is quite possible no doctor had ever even diagnosed him and that he was a person unscathed by status or the lack thereof. He seemed proud to be capable of turning his eyelids inside-out—they were big and pink and thick—and perhaps this trick granted him the power he needed to feel he had some control over his life.

After recess we would return to class and have our science lesson, and then we would go to lunch. In the afternoons we would have a rest period and then a math lesson and another recess, and it would be days, sometimes weeks, before the student would be struck by another epileptic fit. But it always happened, and when it did, it was always the same: The teacher, smaller than the student, would restrain him, while his body convulsed and we watched, in what became a normal routine situation.

The experience taught us that life goes on in the midst of the abnormal. It taught us a lot of things, such as hoping for the best, yet knowing the worst could happen and that if it did, our competent and confident young teacher could handle the situation with ease, and that the student would escape the horror of the moment with his dignity intact.

The student is gone now, and may he rest in peace, knowing that he left us all with vivid memories and valuable lessons of courage, resilience, and gifts.

## Girl Scout Trauma

When I was little, I would stand on a kitchen chair and eat sugar by the spoonful, straight out of the sugar bowl.

"Get out of that sugar bowl, girl!" my mother would yell, and I would down one more lovin' spoonful.

I would leap out of the chair, put my hands on my hips and proclaim, "When I grow up, I'm going to buy a whole pound of sugar and eat it all by myself."

My mother, ever the unnerved one, would just stare at me in fear of what I would do next. I grew up, Mama died, and I never ate that pound of sugar, because adulthood somehow squelched the desire.

People say things have changed, and in many ways they have. As a child, I spent my summer days with my friends at the pool and the adjoining park. Back then they didn't have cameras in parks, because the only people there were screaming, barefoot kids eating Boston Baked Beans and Sweet Tarts and chewing large wads of Bazooka Bubble Gum.

These days, you can't even pick your nose in the park or adjust your wedgie, due to certain unmentionable acts.

Yes, things have changed, but that's not to say that past generations were unscathed. Ironically, it was the Girl Scout experience that traumatized me most. It was bad enough having to flounce around in the green Girl Scout dress with the sash. It was cute back in the Brownie years, but my green sash was lacking in badges, and I never could find my pins.

Oh, if only it had stopped there in the midst of the lame, but my Girl Scout years were the end of my innocence.

One fateful Friday night back in fifth grade, our Girl Scout leaders held a sleepover for us at our regular meeting place, which included a kitchen and several other rooms. The leaders were snoring away by ten, and we had free reign. For weeks, Rita had been promising to tell us "the facts of life," and we eagerly awaited the moment. Rita, at age eleven, was somehow the hormonal equivalent of a twenty-one-year-old.

On the floor of the tiny kitchen, we all gathered wide-eyed around Rita, perched on the ledge of the facts of life. Still being the child who planned to eat a whole pound of sugar when I grew up, I had no idea what the facts of life entailed.

Rita proceeded to tell us in great detail about how she and the preacher's boy often went down underneath the bridge in the tall green grass. Most of the girls seemed impressed, but I was unable to grasp the notion. There was simply no way to integrate such a tale with my dream of eating a pound of sugar.

Around midnight, we gathered 'round while Rita stood in the middle of a circle, snapping her fingers and singing Roger Miller's "King of the Road." I have never recovered from that night, and I now know why they need cameras in parks and trolls underneath bridges.

And then there was the time they took us to the county jail and we saw an encaged woman who thought she was a bird and was squawking and flapping her arms. I'll admit, this was without question the highlight of my Girl Scout years. There was much, much more, but enough is enough.

Suffice it to say I never forced my own daughters to be Girl Scouts. I let them play video games and eat sugar instead.

## "You Did What?"

My mother often said to me, "Didn't you wear that thing *yesterday,* hon?" When I got my first permanent, she said, "Well, I hope you didn't *pay* for that."

In my teenage years I often told her, "My name is not "You Did *What?*"

When I graduated from college, she said, "I cannot believe you graduated from college."

Still I loved her, and she loved me, even though we didn't mush around with each other a whole lot.

Back around 1974 on a Saturday night, my mother was sitting alone in the den with my sister's date, when a Massengill Douche commercial came on TV. My sister was in the bathroom smiling at herself, and I was in the kitchen, spying on my mother while she pretended a douche commercial was not dancing before her eyes in front of my sister's date.

The boy just sat there with a "duh" look on his face, as teenage boys so often do, and my mother sat there with an "I'm going to act normal even if there is a porn commercial on TV while I am alone with this boy. Gad!" It was one of the highlights of my life, and she never got over it.

In today's world I often wonder what my mother would do while sitting alone with one of our dates in the midst of a modern-day porn commercial. I would love to see the look on her face when the Cialis man says, "And if you get an erection that lasts more than four hours, call your doctor immediately."

I wonder how she would respond to the woman who smiles and whispers, "Every woman has little panty leaks from time to time."

I'm not one hundred percent positive, but I like to believe that if she saw the commercial where the maxi pad with wings flies across the den and morphs into a comfy recliner, she would kill the TV with the fireplace poker. But then she would be faced with the dilemma of not getting to watch *As the World Turns* re-runs.

I like to ponder how my mother would cast her vote at the presidential polls. She was a Democrat back when Democrats were Democrats and did not turn on each other in the midst of an opportunity, so that's a hard one to guess.

I like to envision the look on her face while reading my book, particularly the columns that tell about her affinity for L&M cigarettes. She'd probably say, "Well, hon, what in the world are you going to do next? What will the preacher think?"

And I would say, "My name is not 'You Did *What?*' And for your information, the preacher smokes Marlboros."

Yes, my mother was a character, and many of us still miss sitting around her kitchen table, drinking endless cups of coffee, while she was screaming her head off during a Vanderbilt basketball game on the small countertop TV. Basketball was one of her later obsessions.

You know it's bad when the intensive care nurse is trying to blast you out of a coma by giving you the latest Larry Bird stats in the peak of the NBA playoffs.

My mother had a good life. How do I know? Because we still miss her, we still laugh when we remember her, and we always will.

## Olga and Helga

Long ago and far away there lived a group of teenage girls who got bored in the summer of 1975. Back then, cell phones did not exist, the iPad did not exist, and the Internet certainly didn't exist. The only computer in town resided at the local manufacturing plant, and it had a room all to itself because it was big as a barn and loud, too.

And so it seemed the only option for these teenage girls on that steamy day in 1975 was the telephone, the old-fashioned black rotary dial sitting on the table between the twin beds in the upstairs bedroom of one of the girls,' who just happened to live smack dab in the middle of town.

It was the perfect teenage girl bedroom, complete with not only a window seat but also windows for the girls to climb out of late at night and talk to the teenage boys who mysteriously poofed out of a cornfield, or something like that.

But this was the summer of '75, pre-video game era, and the teenage boys were hauling hay or perhaps lifeguarding at the pool. It was mid-July, that time of the summer when the pool had lost its crowd and its appeal, and teenage girls grew weary and bored in the afternoons. Inside, the air conditioner would cool them off, but outside, they were slow and misguided, all because of the humidity, of course.

They were lying around like hound dogs, stretched out all over the floor and on the twin beds, bored out of their gourds, all four of them.

It is hard to say whose idea it was. Perhaps it materialized, just like the teenage boys who knew just when to poof out of the cornfield. But while they were sprawled out all over the place in their Levi's cutoffs complete with white fringe and long tan legs, the black rotary dial seemed to beckon them from the very depth of their souls.

"I know!" one of them said. "Let's call Lance and talk to him in Swedish accents. Let's tell him we're in town visiting our aunt, and that we want him to meet us at Star Market!"

The others agreed. It was immediate, and it was brilliant, and nothing short of a meteor hitting the earth would have stopped Olga and Helga at that particular moment on that hot summer day.

In an instant, Lance was on the other end of the line, and Olga and Helga came to life in yet another poof, just out of the blue. Their accents were not only believable, but also sultry and sexy and Swedish, as only a teenage girl from Tennessee can emulate to perfection. The words, "We saw you and we want you to meet us," just oozed out of their mouths, and Lance was not only hooked but captured, just out of the blue.

The teenage girls hopped onto their bicycles and raced over to the market and went inside, nonchalantly looking at candy bars and chewing gum and Slim Jims. There, standing back beside the Coca-Cola cooler was Lance, trying to look nonchalant himself.

A casual observer would have never suspected that he was on the verge of a Swedish orgy. The teenage girls watched Lance stare at the Cokes, then look over his shoulder to the left and then to the right. They watched him as he began to look slightly puzzled and confused. And they giggled, hard. They left the store giggling and hopped on their bicycles and flew back to the upstairs bedroom of the downtown girl and they giggled on into the night.

They are still giggling somewhere, knowing that inside of them lives an Olga and a Helga, and knowing that on a hot summer day in the middle of the afternoon in 1975, they poofed into town, only for a brief visit, but one that would last a lifetime.

And Lance? Whatever happened to Lance? The girls never knew, but they always heard he was still watching for Olga and Helga, casually looking over his shoulder, first to the left and then to the right, waiting for them to poof before him, just out of the blue.

## The Attic

I went up in my attic yesterday to get the Halloween stuff. I like attics because they tell a story. Somewhere between the Great Pumpkin and Santa Claus lies the story of my life.

There's my Brownie book, my Girl Scout handbook, and my old college textbooks. There's a box of Feltman Brothers gowns that each of my babies wore home from the hospital. There's the box of love letters my husband and I wrote to each other before we were married.

There's a box of Care Bears and Puffalumps and assorted Barbies. The one-armed Baby Shivers has a box all to herself. There is a troll case that contains an assortment of trolls, and I am tempted to open it up and let them out. I love trolls because they are remnants of my own childhood. These trolls are my daughter's, though. New and improved trolls. They'll come around again in twenty more years, and I'll be able to twist, braid, and pile their hair with my grandchildren.

There's the box of cards and letters from when my mother died. Beside it sits a box of important papers from when my grandfather died. Important documents like insurance policies, wills, and medical bills.

Attics are filled with all things legal.

The things that sit in attics are things that we cling to for sentimental reasons. We care deeply about our attic things. They sometimes remind us of how much others care. They may remind us of how hard we struggled. Some of them lie in wait to be used once again: the Brownie handbook, the Feltman Brothers gowns, the Baby Shivers, the family of trolls and their adorable plastic cave.

I used to go up in my granny's attic and prowl around. There was an old trunk of my great-grandmother's that contained embroidered linens, love letters, and old books. At age ninety-three, all the books are old. There was an old family Bible with names like Alonzo and Thaddeus. There was a record of a baby's death: born May 1, 1902; died November 8, 1904. Pneumonia. There were birth certificates, marriage certificates, and death certificates. And there was a box of old love letters that my grandparents wrote to each other before they were married. Pretty good stuff. When I was a child, it bothered me to read the letters, but now I understand.

Yesterday, a sentimental mood settled over me while I was up in the attic, and I plopped down and opened the box of love letters my husband and I wrote each other. It had been years since I'd read them, and I was surprised to feel the way I felt when I first read my grandparents' love letters. It was that "old-fogies-aren't-supposed-to-feel-that-way" feeling. Just as I was getting to the good part, my husband yelled up, "What are you doing up there?"

"I'm dancing with skeletons," I yelled back. "It's Halloween."

"Well, come on down," he said. "Your sister's on the phone, and I'm going to pick up the kids."

Back to the real world. But isn't it nice to know escape is only an attic away?

## The Lucky Pink Shirt

It was the summer of 1978, one of my best summers, as we all have our best summers that stand out for whatever reason. During that particular summer, I remember Bob Seger's "Night Moves" blaring out all over the place, although the song was released in October, 1976, and still resonates today "out past the cornfields where the woods got heavy."

Another great song in the summer of 1978 was Gerry Rafferty's "Baker Street." I remember sitting at the Pizza Hut in my hometown with a sporadic friend here and there, for our group of friends had gone astray two years after high school graduation, as friends often do. Some marry, some go to college, some leave for a faraway land, but back in 1978 past the cornfields where the woods got heavy, many of the old friends stuck around.

Many of them are still there today with children and grandchildren of their own. But somehow I think we all recall the summer of 1978, working on the night moves, "when you just don't seem to have as much to lose, till autumn closes in," and it surely did close in.

Aside from autumn with all its cool change, today it was the lucky pink shirt that got me to thinking about the summer of 1978. I was doing the annual summer/winter clothes exchange, and while I have improved on parting with attire that will never realistically again fit into my wardrobe or benefit my body or my family in any way, there are things I keep from year to year, and I always will.

There are my children's T-shirts from the very first Woodard Wildcat Walk—definite keepers. There is that denim embroidered shirt from 1976, compliments of my mother, complete with my name and little pink and blue flowers on the back that I will always cherish. There's that dark seafoam-green dress my mother made me in high school. Back then a lot of our mothers sewed a lot of our clothes, and this one just stands out for no particular reason.

There is the dress I wore to my mother's funeral in June 1987—a maternity dress at that—and there is a dress from 1998 that I love, simply because of the muted hues of red and blue and cream. It reminds me of some type of French painting. I am too ignorant to speak of French art or French anything, but I do know the dress worked for me and that I will always love it too much to say goodbye.

But nothing compares to the pastel pink shirt of the summer of 1978. I bought the shirt at The Limited, and it was a pale cotton, my favorite material, and it had a small collar with small white buttons on the front. It was a normal shirt by all appearances, but during the summer of 1978, I noticed that whenever I wore the shirt, things turned out particularly well, so much so that I began to call it "my lucky shirt."

The summer passed, as summers always do, but the shirt remained the same. As I moved around during the college years, I took the shirt with me wherever I went, and sometimes my roommates would borrow it. In the spring of 1980, the pastel pink cotton shirt with the small white collar and the little white buttons was the perfect pick for my roommate who was going out on her first date with a new young man, a potential keeper.

I told her, "This shirt will bring you luck—I know that for a fact."

She wore the shirt, ended up marrying the man, and I have no idea where she is today. But I do know that she is still married to him and that they have children and that their marriage has endured the test of time thus far.

Do I still have that shirt? Yes, I do. I surely do. It has brought me so much luck that I cannot possibly ask for any more, but it's nice just knowing it's still there and that for people all over our country, the perfect summer is just around the corner, just waiting on that pink shirt and that sweet moment in time with "Night Moves" playing in the background.

## My House Is Right Down That Street

My sister calls, excited. "It's snowing down here. The rooftops are covered, and there's already an inch of snow on the ground!"

I look outside at the cold gray skies and see nothing. I stare harder and suddenly a flake falls, then another. Soon it is snowing hard, and I call my friend. She says it is not snowing at her house. While we are talking, my husband calls to tell me it is snowing at his office. I call my friend back, and still, it is not snowing at her house. I tell her to look hard.

"I see it!" she says. "It's snowing at our house!"

My husband comes home and builds a roaring fire while the ground turns white. Deep in the mode of winter, I hunker down at the computer in my daughter's bedroom and click on the local weather for an update. I see they have my hometown square on the skycam, and I stare at the angle and the beauty and the wonder and the presence of my past, right before my eyes. I right-click and put the picture on my desktop background.

There's the First National Bank building. There's Ledbetter's to the left, and there's the statue of Davy Crockett. There's The Bootery over to the right, and there's the gazebo that replaced the courthouse they tore down back in the '70s.

There is a pale neon green glow cast over the town square, and there is a fortress of trees standing tall and proud and strong above the buildings. I have never viewed it from this angle.

The glow is angelic, heavenly, in the night skycam picture. I lean forward and look closely at the street beside the bank, and my mind travels northward. My house is right down that street. I'm almost home.

I stare at the picture some more and remind myself not to think too hard. Just feel. Just look at the picture and stare at what is there and what used to be there and what might still be there. Understatement is good, I think. It is good that I cannot see my house in this picture, so that I may draw my own conclusions.

The streets are black, shiny, and wet, and the ground is white underneath the halo glow of the town square on which a neon pastel Christmas light shines. But my eyes are drawn to the street that leads north, and I travel outside the picture.

There, just up the road, are the steps to my house. I climb them slowly so that I can take it all in. The steps are wet with snow, and the swing hangs still on this silent night. The columns of the front porch are intact, and the light is on in the living room.

I stand at the door of my house and turn to look back at the street of my hometown. There is no need to knock or go inside. I just want to stand here for a minute and watch. Take it all in now that I am old enough to appreciate and understand it. From the darkness of the front porch, I watch the cars drive by on the damp night street. The people have been to the store to get coffee and milk and sugar, and they are headed home to the safety and comfort and warmth of their own fireplaces.

I walk back down the steps and feel the snowflakes land on the tip of my nose, and I head south down the street and step back into the picture.

There is magic in the snow. Be still and look hard and you will see it.

## Childhood Girlfriends

I had dozed off around nine p.m., when the phone rang a week ago.

"This is Becky," she said, as if I wouldn't know. I'd heard that voice all my life. "A bunch of us are going to meet for lunch on Saturday, and we wanted you to come with us."

"I don't think so," I said in a fuzzy voice. "Let me get back to you." Immediately, I conjured up lame excuses not to go. These were people from my childhood, people from another time and another place—my hometown. I was tired of looking back. The thought of spending time reminiscing over the way things were versus the way things are made me bury my head under my pillow. "Oohing" and "aahing" over pictures of kids who all looked the same. Little League, prom, graduation, wedding, and even grandchildren.

I decided to stay home and pull weeds.

Pulling weeds has a way of clearing my head and working the kinks out of my system.

I was murdering the crab grass, mindlessly thinking about my childhood girlfriends, when a thought hit me. More than one thought, actually.

These were the people who showed up at my mother's funeral. They brought food, sent cards and flowers, and stayed in touch. We gave each other wedding and baby showers. We went all the way through school together, some of us all the way back to kindergarten. We'd gone full circle—from pudgy little bodies at age five to pudgy big bodies at age forty-plus. I could still see these girls in their plaid jumpers and knee socks and Buster Brown shoes. There was Ann, flashing an ear-to-ear grin with no front teeth. I remembered them in their Brownie uniforms and later, their white go-go boots. I remembered when the pudgy little bodies were transformed by the essence of puberty, peaking around our eighth grade year. I remembered our first boy-girl hayride and snuggling up under the hay with boys of different shapes and sizes, who were even crazier than we were. I remembered "American Pie" and Screaming Yellow Zonkers and the sackful of notes I saved from my eighth grade year: "Save me some bubblegum for basketball practice, okay?" "Do you think Tina's hair looks good?" "Do you think John likes me?" "Are you going to Cindy's party?" "Susan just moved in here and took over the place." "Vicky is so little and cute. I hope she gets fat someday." "I think Daniel likes Cathy." "Emily's cat died this morning and she ran out of social studies class." "Save me a seat at the pep rally." "Mr. Jones makes us run too much. Do you think you'll start out

Friday night?" "Mr. Green is two hundred eighty years old. He never even knew when that desk flew out the window!" "Throw me a Jolly Rancher when he's not looking."

I ripped out a thistle, changed my mind, and went to lunch with my old friends on Saturday.

Outwardly, we "oohed" and "aahed" over our kids. We trashed our ex-es and bashed our old boyfriends.

Inwardly, we took inventory of gray hair, diamonds, career levels, and social status. We were, after all, human.

After Saturday, I realized my circle of childhood friends was a treasure I had taken for granted. In all probability, I will continue to do so, but they will forgive me because that is what we do.

Although I rarely see them, I know they are there, and that is one of the great comforts of my life.

## Music, Sweet Music

The year was 1967, and my favorite part of school was music class. We sang lots of songs, but my favorite was "Red River Valley." Back in fourth grade, before the peer pressure kicks in and while the innocence remains, children sing with gusto, and our class had lots of gusto that year. At Thanksgiving we sang "Over the River and Through the Woods," and at Christmas we sang "Santa Claus is Coming to Town," like nobody's business.

I could tell our music teacher was so impressed with us that she spent her time plotting and planning how to take us out on the road, perhaps to Broadway, and let us perform. We would hit the road on a tour bus and be on TV in New York City and wave and smile and blow kisses to our classmates left behind. We would send our condolences to the principal and wish him the best.

Yes, music class was the place where we sang in perfect harmony, but in all fairness the credit goes to the teacher, who was a cross between Aretha Franklin, Oprah, and B.B. King. Simply put, when God sprinkled love into her heart, He gave her a triple dose, and that was why, when we walked into her designated spot, she smiled at each and every one of us as if a class of ten thousand angels had entered through her door.

But she didn't even have a door. She had a small space in a corner of the cafeteria to the left of the stage, but it didn't seem to matter to her or to us, because when she sat down at her piano, that thing was rocking like a baby in a new mama's arms. I'm not positive, but I believe our music teacher was the one who taught Jerry Lee Lewis how to shake, rattle, and roll. I think he stole "Chantilly Lace" from her repertoire, but it's only a suspicion, and she wouldn't care anyway because to her, music was a gift to be shared and experienced to the fullest. The more she gave, the more she had and she had a whole lot.

Being a fourth-grader and nine years old in 1967, I was not aware of the radical change that was happening in our country. I knew nothing of civil rights, the women's movement, or the Vietnam War. The only clue I had witnessed that change was in the air was a poster of

Snoopy holding a peace sign, and the caption read, "Make love, not war." Of course, I did not know what that meant, either, and I did not care because I was in fourth grade, and I cared about my family, my friends, our poodle Tinkerbell, and head-banging to "Red River Valley."

I was not aware of children who were "different," because back then there were no "different" children in public schools. But I did notice, out of the corner of my eye, while walking to school each morning, that a new red brick building was being erected beside our very own school. It never occurred to me to ask what it was. It never occurred to me that it was a school for the "different" children, because I had no concept of such a thing until one very unforgettable day, a day that would leave a permanent impression on my classmates and me for the rest of our lives—a day that would shake up the innocence of even a fourth-grader.

It was a normal day at first, and there we were in music class singing "Red River Valley," while I pictured myself beside a campfire somewhere out West, wearing some type of prairie girl garb and stuffing s'mores into my mouth. While we were singing and while our teacher was banging the ivories and the pedal in her usual style, the "different" children walked in or were wheeled in, one by one, led by their teacher. They just stood there and watched us sing, stayed for a while, and then they walked out in a line and went next door to "their" school. My classmates and I didn't seem to process the experience as anything out of the ordinary, because our hearts were young and sweet and innocent and naturally accepting of others, as young children are.

Our teacher was not so unfazed. As soon as the last one walked out the front door of our school, she started sobbing and weeping and wailing like nothing I had ever seen or heard before. She crossed her arms and laid her head down on them and banged them up and down the piano scale, creating a song of grief and despair that was so desolate I can still remember the tune. She was singing the blues that day, the bona fide blues, and I challenge anyone on this planet to match the depth of ache she felt in her heart that day, for her heart was surely broken. It was broken for the children who were "different," and perhaps it was broken for all the things that were wrong in the world at that time. She had a moment where her cross was too much to bear, and we were the beneficiaries of it, because we witnessed for the first time that change was in the air for us all, and that none of us had any guarantees.

Our lives were changed that day when the heart of an angel burst right before our eyes, and we were blessed to have her in her lives. I don't know where she is today, but I like to imagine she is somewhere in a large room of her very own, banging the ivories on her baby grand with a marble floor beneath her feet, surrounded by the innocence of small children, both normal and different.

## Some Enchanted Evening

My cousin Margaret has a gift for bringing the past to life. Every word from her mouth paints a picture that is pure and true, for Margaret is the most honest person I have ever known. Without effort, the sound of her voice and the words from her mouth bring sweet tears to my eyes.

"Margaret," I say, "you should read audio books. You have the most expressive voice I've ever heard."

"Oh hon," she laughs, "thank you for saying that. But my old body's too tired to try anything new."

Margaret is a rare link to my past. She is my mother's first cousin, and through the years, she tells me bits and pieces about their younger days. When Cousin Margaret speaks, my mother dances back to life, and I can see her as a young woman, embarking on the decisions that brought me into this world.

"One night back in 1950," says Margaret, "I was spending the night with your mama, and we were stretched out across the bed in the front bedroom looking at magazines. Your mama had just returned from a date with your daddy, and we were listening to 'Some Enchanted Evening' on the Victrola. Your mama said, 'I'm going to marry that man,' and we giggled into the night."

Here I am. Mama's dead, and love is blind, and who's to say what's wrong or right?

If Rodgers and Hammerstein hadn't written "Some Enchanted Evening," I might not be here. Who knows? But then Mama might have been swept away by another song such as "Someone to Watch Over Me," or my favorite oldie, "Moon River."

I'm glad it was "Some Enchanted Evening" that propelled my parents down the aisle and into the marital unknown. It's that way the song succumbs to the seemingly inevitable that melts my heart:

Sometimes you just know. For better or worse, wrong or right, you just know. It hit me back in 1982, when my future husband had to embark on his journey back home at two in the morning, and I asked, "Would you like a piece of toast?"

"Yes," he said. "That would be nice."

And it was at that moment that I said to myself, "I'm going to marry that man." It had nothing to do with the toast. I don't know how I knew, I just did. And Rodgers and Hammerstein knew romantic analysis was futile.

Here's to old songs, enchanted evenings, young hearts, and unasked questions. Without these gifts, our lives might not exist.

## Mamas and Trains

Most people have a soft spot for mamas and trains, it seems. This is one of the thoughts that crossed my mind while walking in the park today, all by myself. I usually walk with a friend, but after all these years, I took the plunge and decided I was big enough and old enough to go it alone, and I made it home safely.

I always think about my mama on June 2, because it is the anniversary of her death. Twenty-five years ago today, she departed from this earthly realm on a day much like today: sunny and cool with a mild breeze rustling through the tender leaves on the trees of early June. A lot has happened in those twenty-five years—too much to tell and no desire to tell it, for two of the lessons learned are that there are places we only have to visit once and life is not always a walk in the park.

But sometimes it is.

Another lesson I have recently learned is not to stand in the middle of a railroad track if there is any inkling of a train on the horizon. In other words, I now pay close attention to my gut feeling and I never question it anymore, because a gut feeling is always right. I wish I had learned that lesson twenty-five years ago rather than in the past nine months, but that's not the way it worked out for me. I'm just thankful to have learned the lesson, period.

Another lesson I have learned is to use my courage, for we all have courage, but few of us make the most of this gift, because it feels scary to think of the consequences of saying and doing the things we yearn to do. On the other hand, we disappoint ourselves if we do not use our courage merely because we are afraid of offending people we don't even admire or wish to spend time with.

And since I have to live with myself for the rest of my life, I decided to go with my own beliefs and take chances. I have learned that the world will not end if I am afraid.

Truth is, the world does not even care. But I care, and my close friends and family members care, and that is what matters to me.

This Thursday evening, on June 7, 2012, my friend Tim Yeager and I will perform some of our original music in public, and I have no idea how this will turn out. It is scary but exciting, and the worst thing that could happen is if I ran off the stage screaming, or if the piano somehow fell on top of somebody. While I do not think those things will happen, I'm going to take a chance, because of all the lessons I have learned since my mama's death twenty-five years ago, the most important one was to take a chance.

We'll see what happens.

# SOUTHERN PRIDE, PREJUDICE, AND RELIGION

## Hell

Southern towns are laced with church signs, and ours is no exception. Recently, I spotted this admonition on the sign outside a local church: Don't wait for the hearse to take you to church.

Is this supposed to be INSPIRING? Come on, people, we can do better than this. For example:

- Jesus loves you, but that's about it.
- Bring your children up in the nurture and admonition of the Lord, and they will move to California.
- For remember, the very hairs of your head have roots, and you need a highlight.
- Hell's hotter than a hog pen in July.
- Pray without preaching.
- Why are people unwilling to admit they are wrong? BECAUSE THEY BELIEVE THEY ARE RIGHT.

My favorite church sign is on Interstate 65, somewhere close to Birmingham: Go to church or the Devil will get you.

Mind you, I think church signs have merit, and I attend church regularly myself. But I believe God has a sense of humor, and I also know that church isn't the only place to find God.

Maybe I'm wrong, but I suspect God grows weary of clichés and pontification. I believe he welcomes new twists on old themes as well as the average reader. New and improved signs such as these might just allow him to sit back and breathe a little easier:

- A catfish a day keeps the Devil away.
- His eye is on the sparrow 'cause he's tired of watching you.
- Because you're vile, I walk the aisle.
- Pride cometh before a cavity search.

Most of us fear Hell and have perceptions of fire and brimstone and a grinning Devil with a wagging tail, holding a pitchfork and getting ready to spear it straight through our hearts. But wait, there's more! Hell is a place where the river runs dry and the tulips are black as a crow. And Hell's connotation varies according to one's nature and profession. Hell for English teachers is no red pens and double negatives scrawled all over the wall, a pit where the milkshakes boil and the beers run dry, and you're always craving a cigarette, but they ain't got none.

When I was a child, I spake as a child, and I still do. I used to ask, "Where is Hell, Mama?"

"Well, hon, I don't know," she'd say. "Just leave me alone for a little while and we'll talk about it later."

Five minutes later I'd go back into the kitchen and ask, "Mama, you never did tell me where Hell was. Where is it? If it's down in the ground, how do you get there? Is there a big slide or something like they have out at the park? Does the Devil really have a pitchfork and horns? Do you think I'll go to Hell, Mama? Will I? Will I?"

"Well, hon, just leave me alone for a little while, and we'll talk about it later. *As the World Turns* is almost off, and then you can go to the store with me. I need you to run in and get me some L&M's, and if the preacher sees you, tell him they're for your daddy."

"But Daddy's in *England*, Mama. And if I lie I'll go to Hell. Do you think I'm going to Hell, Mama? Do you?"

"Well, hon, good night—if you don't leave me alone, I believe I will go insane. Why don't you run out and play in your sandbox for a little while. Or go read *Little Black Sambo*. You love that book."

That settled it. If Mama wasn't worried about Hell, then I wasn't going to worry about it either. I went to my sandbox and later read *Little Black Sambo* and later still went with Mama to Star Market to buy her some L&M's, because I was bolder than she was, and I still am.

Now my own children ask me where Hell is and I tell them it's right here on God's green earth, in the heart of an addict and the soul of a liar. Hell lies in the absence of our belief in God's grace, His greatest gift of all.

Now why couldn't Mama have said that?

## The Creature

I have always been blessed with people who exist merely to save my soul.

Many moons ago, when I was pregnant with my first child, a certain religious group knocked on my door and informed me there was no such thing as a burning Hell. According to them, a burning Hell was mentioned nowhere in the Bible. I was, however, requested to donate all my personal savings to their church and go door to door with them for the rest of my life.

I chose Hell.

The absence of a burning Hell was completely foreign to everything I'd ever been taught in church. I'd been trained to have the utmost respect for a burning Hell, because that was most likely where I would spend eternity, shoveling coal.

Several years later, when I was pregnant with my third child, I was planting onions in my garden when yet another ticket to Heaven presented itself. It was a gorgeous sunny day in April, full of promise and hope. The birds were harmonizing, the tulips were blooming, and the preacher was tapping his toes. Of all the nerve, he was standing in *my* garden with his arms crossed! I had visited his church, "the one and only true church," a few times, and had chosen to go elsewhere when my daughter kept referring to him as "the creature." She was a smart little thing.

I learned a long time ago that if you pretended everything was all right, people would leave you alone.

"I'm worried about you," said the creature, as he stuck an onion in the ground.

"Well, I'm doing just fine," I replied, flashing a smile and holding onto my belly. This was a great sympathy tactic upon which I relied during all my pregnancies.

The creature lingered and planted on. He was such a generous soul. I could tell he was thinking, "She's a little slow. How am I ever going to reach her? How can I sear her simple spirit?"

Little did he know I was playing dumb to get rid of him. I wanted to plant my own onions.

I kept planting and pulling an occasional weed. Suddenly, I came up with the perfect plan. Diversion was yet another tactic I had mastered.

I wiped my brow and looked concerned. "You know," I said thoughtfully, "I have tried and tried to get those neighbors over there to quit serving beer to their fourteen-year-old twin sons. On weekends and holidays, they sit out on their deck, fire up the keg, and offer fifty bucks to the fastest guzzler. Even their Chihuahua, Corona, gets plastered! Last week, he passed out and fell off the deck. After the contest ends, those next-door drunkards guide their wobbling teens to bed and then sneak back out to the deck to smoke some of that *wacky weed* they grow in their garden. See, there it is, hidden between the corn and the sunflowers."

The creature was mesmerized. He squinted and stepped toward their garden, his eyes oozing with opportunity. Meanwhile, I was smelling like a rose.

"If you'll excuse me," I said, "I need to go lie down. The baby is wedged in a knot."

"Of course, of course," the creature replied, as he stroked his chin and stared at the neighbors' garden. The salvation quotient was gaining every minute.

I never knew if the creature approached the neighbors or not. And the onions? Well, mine were crisp, succulent, and tasty. But the creature had planted his onions upside down.

Maybe I'll see them in Hell.

## Four Rows of Okra, Part 1

*What begins on one day will end on another.*

—Newton's Fourth Law of Motion

It all started last Thursday, when I was Oxford-bound to visit our daughter in Mississippi. My bags were packed and I was ready to go—leaving in a Red Bug when an engine-shaped light popped up and my Bug started humming another tune: "Take Me to the Mothership."

And so I did, and they kept my Bug until Tuesday. I picked it up and on the way home, the light reappeared, and my Bug started humming again, and the very next morning I was back at the Volkswagen dealership for a new diagnosis and repair.

Aside from the canceled trip to Oxford, I was secretly glad the light came on because a trip to the dealership means a shuttle trip to the mall, where I happened to hit the sale of the century at a large department store. It was one of those days every woman has at some point in her lifetime: everything is fifty percent off, everything fits, and some items are seventy-five percent off. While I am not a big shopper, I'll admit I did experience a mild case of "shopper's high," where an inner voice whispers, "The children? Ha! They don't need to go to college anyway. You've done your duty. Buy the whole store! You deserve it!"

I was feeling the love. Gone were the thoughts of my beloved poodle, Tinkerbell, dead from rotten old age back in 1976. And that boyfriend who left me for divinity school back in 1981? Good riddance! Ditto that other guy back in 1976. There at the check-out counter, I was in a place where I knew my mama was in Heaven, cloud-hopping with Granny and Tinkerbell, and I was free of any worry, period. I was even able to assure myself that my precious grandbaby Lily was safe and secure and not standing in the middle of a crowded street in front of a large hungry baboon.

An added bonus was the woman in front of me with the irresistible personality. She was attractive, she was funny, she was inquisitive, she was edgy and opinionated, and she was Southern to the core. The woman beside her said, "Next time she goes to the clearance rack, I want her to pick out my bling!"

It was then that the woman and I checked out each other's bling, and she held a small black top up and said, "I just hate it when these things are too tight against my bust. Don't you?"

I said, "Well, I'm a teacher, and our county has a student dress code policy, and at school, I don't wear things like that."

"Well, I have never in my life seen such cleavage as these young girls want to show!" she said. "Do you see a lot of cleavage at your school?" she asked.

"We deal with it," I said. "We don't let them show cleavage. We don't let them wear those little feathers in their hair, either."

"Well, why on earth NOT?" she asked. "What in the world is wrong with feathers? That is carrying it entirely too far! What has happened to common sense? What would those little feathers hurt?"

"Well, if we let them wear feathers, next thing you know they'll be wearing two-foot blue and green peacock feathers in their hair, and that is what we refer to as a DISTRACTION. Things can get out of hand before you know it."

She eyed me and asked, "What county do you teach in?"

"Maury County," I replied. "Maury County Public Schools."

Until that moment, I thought I had witnessed an eye roll or two in my lifetime. Between my mother, my husband, my children, my students, and my own self, I did not think the eye roll could be outdone. But this woman did the impossible: she gave me the most humongous eye roll I'd ever seen, and then she said, "Maury County? Talk about four rows of okra! There's a world of difference between Williamson County and Maury County—an entire UNIVERSE, in fact!"

"And do you know why that is?" I said. "It's because NOBODY FROM WILLIAMSON COUNTY IS FROM THE SOUTH! They're all from California and Boston and even parts of Canada."

The sales lady was looking at us in a confused and slightly concerned manner. I could tell she was thinking, "This is not a discussion panel, it is a checkout register, and people are looking at you and waiting in line behind you." Still, I could tell she was intrigued. For one thing, she had a Northern accent.

She rang the Southern bling lady up and told her she saved five hundred fifty-four bucks and gave her a coupon. Then she rang me up and said I saved one hundred twenty-eight bucks, and I felt slightly deflated, not about the lesser savings, but about the "four rows of okra" comment. For one thing, I wish I'd thought of it. And for another thing, it hit a nerve.

But hey, this is life, and every day a nerve gets hit. And the okra? Well, guess what, Miss Busty Bling?

At least we know what okra is when we see it. And as for the feathers, well, regardless of opinion, you can't always get what you want. But if you try sometime, you might just find you get what you need.

It's a hard lesson for us all, but we all have to learn it at some point.

## Four Rows of Okra, Part 2

After parting ways with Miss Busty Bling, who had seriously insulted our county with her "four rows of okra" comment at the check-out counter in the large department store, I called Rafael and asked him to come and get me so that I could get my car back and drive it back to the mall, where I would continue my wild shopping spree in the store where everything fit and was at least fifty percent off.

Rafael was out to lunch, so another guy called and said, "I'm coming to pick you up in a black Jaguar outside the food court."

"Okay," I said.

A voice in the back of my mind asked how he knew I would be in the food court, but it was only a blip on the screen, and I dismissed it as I popped a sample of honeyseed chicken into my mouth and walked out the door. Sure enough, the black Jaguar was there, and I hopped into the front seat. The driver was a young man with dark hair and as we sped along I realized the car was unmarked. "You are the driver from the Volkswagen dealership, aren't you?" I asked.

"Yes," he said, and I was not afraid. Somehow I knew this kid had no intention of picking up a woman more than twice his age and taking her to parts unknown, yet I did have my purse in whack position, just in case. He dropped me off, and I headed back to the mall and parked in front of the magic store.

Turns out I was no longer on a roll. The clothes I liked were not on sale, and I got stuck inside a shirt with a built-in camisole that would have challenged Houdini himself. After my escape I went back to the food court.

Tired from my excursion, my egg roll and I sat down at a table in the sunlight section across from Yoga Mama and her little girl. Yoga Mama dangled a cucumber in front of her daughter, who shook her head in wistful resignation as she stared at my egg roll.

I could tell she was thinking, "Why does my mom have to be Yoga Mama? Why does she have to slip her ninety-five-pound body into her yoga clothes and wear them to the mall and dangle sliced cucumbers in front of my mouth? Why can't she be like that other mama over there—the one that ate five rounds of free samples and is now inhaling an egg roll like the end of the world has come?"

I sensed the party was over, and it was time to go home. I stepped out of the food court and into the one-hundred-degree heat and walked toward my car. After circling the parking lot four times, I began to wonder where it was. After eight times, I decided I might have parked it somewhere else. To be brutally honest, I was lost. Flat out, acting-like-a-man lost. And just like a man, I kept walking around trying to look cool and nonchalant at all costs, and then I gave up and went and stood on a grassy hill and looked down at the parking lot below.

I didn't feel worried, but a loud voice in my head laughed and said, "You look really stupid." To make matters worse, I had a flashback from the previous week, when a co-worker said to me, "You're just like that old girl from Arkansas. You don't even know where you are half the time."

Suddenly, a little old lady pulled up and said, "Are you lost, honey? Have you lost your car?"

"Yes," I said.

"Well, if you trust me to help you find it, hop in, and I'll take you," she said.

"Okay," I said.

And so we circled the parking lot endless times as she told me bits and pieces about her life. Let's just say we sort of bonded during that brief time, even though we did not find my car. I thanked her and asked her just to let me out at the security desk.

Sure enough, the security people said somebody loses a car every day, and one woman even lost her husband. Just as my dignity was returning, the little old lady came running toward the desk saying, "I found it! I found it!"

"I'll just go with her," I told the security people, and we ran out the door. We drove in circles for about ten more minutes talking about bits and pieces of our lives, when suddenly my car appeared.

"There it is!" I screamed. She slammed on her brakes, and I thanked her and wrote down her name and got into my car and drove home.

On my way home, I thought about her some more and realized I sort of missed her and wondered if I would ever see her again. She wasn't the type who would say, "You don't even know where you are half the time."

She is the type who would say, "Honey, are you lost? Have you lost your car?" and then she would take you to find it.

I met a lot of mamas that day, including myself. Out of all of us, I admired her the most and liked her best. I think she may have grown up in a county with a whole field of okra, and I will always be thankful for the day she rescued my car and me.

## You Can't Make Me Feel Stoopid Without My Persimmon

When the going gets tough, the tough get going and suddenly every cliché you have ever heard in your entire lifetime begins to pop into your head and make its way into your location of stress, whether it be work, play, home, or shoveling up roadkill on the side of the road to sell in a secret location behind the Farmer's Market.

For most people in my world, times are hard. People are dealing with everything from the economy to unannounced flatulence, to looking in the mirror and realizing you could look exactly like James Dean if it weren't for those stupid Dumbo ears on the side of your head.

A visitor in my workplace asked me after dropping in unannounced, "Just what exactly is your point?" The words rang a faint but familiar bell, one that I heard from someone long ago, and then I remembered it was my editor. I am actually thankful for my editor, because he has saved me on many occasions from babbling like a complete idiot to rambling like a slight dingbat. I am not thankful for the uninvited guest, because I felt her intention was not to save me, but to mangle the remnant of dignity she detected in me. It didn't work out for her. We parted ways and as they say, "Within every crisis lies an opportunity."

Hence my new slogan inspired directly from my unannounced and uninvited guest: YOU CAN'T MAKE ME FEEL STOOPID WITHOUT MY PERSIMMON.

If I'd known she was coming, not only would I have baked a cake, I'd have worn the slogan on a T-shirt. Thing is, I didn't come up with the slogan till I met her. The whole thing got me to thinking about my lifelong desire to write greeting cards and slogans for T-shirts, so I do have to thank the wench for jolting my memory. Here are a few of my ideas:

- I have no idea what you've been through, and you have no idea what I've been through, so just shut up.
- I can't wait till I grow up and get shriveled and old like you!
- If you're going to do it, do it while you're still alive.
- Everything I know I learned from soap operas.
- Just eat a potato and go back to bed.
- Comfortably dumb

In my former line of work, we sometimes dreamt of new careers, such as sitting on the couch and staring out the window for the rest of our lives, or picking up pine cones and selling them to elves at Christmas. Personally, I toyed with the thought of being a massage therapist, if for no other reason than to have a business card that says, "I used to peruse rubrics with my friends; now I rub their bodies."

Yes, it's true that within every crisis lies an opportunity. And while my uninvited and unannounced guest and I will not be taking road trips together, I do appreciate the fact that she reminded me of some of the things I want to do when I grow up, and most importantly, she reminded me of what I never want to be when I grow up.

Hopefully, she learned something from me, as well.

## Mulletville

There is a large store in town that I typically avoid on weekends because it is packed with people from parts unknown, and that scares me. On Saturdays, this place is a mullet-head tattoo festival. It is a commercialized county fair on a Saturday night with no curtain in front of the girlie show. Problem is, no one wants to look at the girls because the tattoos on their beer guts are stretched out and faded from the gestation period of baby Montana, who is standing on his head in the shopping cart with his four younger siblings while his pink-headed mama is checking out the alien that kidnapped Michelle Obama on the cover of *The National Enquirer*.

But the thing that annoys me most about this place on weekends is the non-handicapped people who plant themselves on the motorized handicapped shopping carts when they are not handicapped. They are SUPERSIZED. I know they are not handicapped because I watch them climb out of their cars and walk into the store on their own two legs. I see them when they look from left to right to make sure no one's looking, and I'm watching when they plop down on the electric scooter for a slow ride through the food section in Mulletville.

This is just wrong. It's like Michael Phelps parking in the handicapped zone, or singing "I Can See Clearly Now" to Stevie Wonder. This is like whispering a deep dark secret into the ear of Helen Keller. This is GLUTTONY, the fattest of sins!

While I'm reading the label on a Metamucil can, here comes Orca on an electric tricycle, and she's downing a large chocolate shake from the fast food arcade. While I'm studying the content of the Flaxseed horse pills, she's smiling at a box of Ding Dongs.

While I'm trying to put a large box of Cheerios in my shopping cart, she's sitting in the middle of the aisle, clutching a large bag of generic Froot Loops.

I make my getaway and escape to the produce section, where she's nowhere in sight, and I breathe a sigh of relief, knowing that my shopping journey has almost come to an end and that I will soon be on my way home. I toss a bag of Fuji apples and a bag of almonds into my cart and race over to the checkout line and come to a screeching halt when I discover Orca is in front of me and Shamu is behind me! I am trapped inside my greatest pet peeve, and all I can do is pretend not to care.

But it gets worse. There is a nice young man, a Marine, in fact, in front of Orca, and he is kindly unloading her groceries and lavishing her with sympathy and compassion all the while. I watch and wait while he piles up her load of Devil Squares, pork rinds, potato chips, orange soda, and other items. While she is sitting there on her throne of gluttony, she rips open the box of Devil Squares and starts munching away, and just when the young Marine thinks he is finished, she tells him there is more food underneath her cart. I look down and sure enough, there are two frozen pizzas perched on top of her left foot, and there is major junk spilling out from down under.

Finally, she is finished, and I watch as three employees wheel her loot out of the store and load it into her car. It is not fair. Orca gets a white knight, and I get a dirty look from the check-out girl.

Such is life in Mulletville.

## Tunica Granny

Talk about contrast. Sam's Town in Tunica, Mississippi, sits in the middle of a cotton field the size of Rhode Island. Neon versus nature at its best. Big bucks versus poverty. Sin versus salvation. Gambling versus lifelessness.

If life is not a gamble, then what is it?

Some believe gambling is wrong. What's wrong with taking a chance and having some fun? What's wrong with winning? What's wrong with losing? What's wrong with turning a cotton field into a casino?

Gambling, Jack Daniel's, and Hershey Bars share a common catch. Each requires perspective and boundaries. The inability or unwillingness to operate within these boundaries renders these pleasures unethical and wrong.

Gambling is a game that can inflict damage, if not played properly. Can the same not be said of life?

If gambling is a sin, many senior citizens are headed way down south—a lot deeper than Mississippi. It may not be much hotter there, but it sure won't be as much fun. The slot machines in Hell might spit out barbecued poker chips. Or maybe they'll spew out sizzling quarters that produce the blisters and pain a gambler deserves. Ouch.

Tunica is a nest for retirees. A love nest, apparently. If these seniors feel any qualms about gambling, they hide it well. Perhaps they have resolved the conflict, if they ever felt it in the first place.

I've only gambled a couple of times, but I've noticed that women play the slots, and men play craps or blackjack.

After my Tunica slot fest, I went into the restroom to wash the nickel stain off my hands. There at the sink stood a silver fox, washing her hands with a dollar bill clenched between her teeth. She was the picture of confidence and stature, and suddenly it hit me. I was in the presence of a Tunica Granny.

I have a mushy place in my heart for grannies, and my motto has always been "If Granny's doing it, it must be all right." In this Delta den of iniquity, there are Tunica Grannies all over the place.

I like to watch people having fun, as long as they're being honest and not hurting anyone. In Tunica, I witnessed some red-hot fun.

My other gambling adventure took place in Las Vegas. There I saw contrast of a different sort. Spewing volcano versus sinking ship. Free buffet versus cheap sex. Hoover Dam versus lost souls. Perhaps it's the abuse of gambling that has led them down this path. Or maybe they just live too close to California.

I like Tunica better. It's smaller, safer, and it's in the South. The heat ain't dry in Tunica. It's thick and steamy and sultry. I'll bet fifty bucks Tunica will never become another Las Vegas. Maybe even a hundred.

Tunica appears to be one hundred percent cotton. And when them cotton fields get rotten, you can't pick very much cotton. But if you play your cards right, you might just get lucky and beat the snout off a boll weevil.

## Quilts

Here in the South, there's just something comforting about a quilt. Even as I sit and write this column in the middle of a hot August night, I am wrapped up in an old patchwork quilt my mother made for me. Some of the pieces of the cotton dresses from my childhood are torn and tattered, but the edges she scalloped by hand are still distinctively intact.

Toward the end of my mother's life, quilting became her hobby. She and her two best friends would sit in the den in front of the fireplace and hand-stitch quilts on the frame my grandfather built for her.

Quilters know they are passing on something that will endure for generations. Like a handwritten letter from the war, a handmade quilt is a gift from the heart, a piece of love with many a fingerprint stamped upon it. And although the particular quilt I am wrapped in now is tattered and torn from constant use, my other quilts are preserved. To me, they are sacred.

At the foot of the bed in the room where I write lies a quilt that a friend made for my daughter when she left for college four years ago. It is a bittersweet comfort to look at the quilt and to wrap myself up in it from time to time and remind myself that unlike life, the quilt has remained the same, like an old-timey song.

Just like my mother, the friend died an untimely death, and when I look at the quilt folded sweetly on my daughter's bed, I am reminded that a part of our friend lives on and is here to cradle us in the middle of the night or during a Sunday afternoon nap. This particular quilt is made of soft, colorful squares of flannel on one side—wildflowers and pastel plaids and clouds in shades of yellow, red, green, and blue. But the backside is even more special because it is made of denim from blue jeans that my children wore throughout the years. Just like Bob Dylan, I get "tangled up in blue" in the middle of the night, and this quilt from a friend is a mere representation of both the metaphor and the reality.

When my grandmother got cancer back in 1982, I visited her every day. One day she led me into the front bedroom and opened a blanket chest that I had never looked inside, which was unusual because I was a curious child, who had explored every nook and cranny inside my grandparents' house. But there was something regal about the blanket chest that sat in the corner of the front bedroom. Like an old safe, it seemed to say, "Look but don't touch." And so I never did.

But on that day, Granny took me into the front bedroom and opened the chest and pulled out a cream-colored quilt that was appliquéd with pink butterflies. It was old, but unmarred, just like Granny. It was beautiful and perfectly preserved. "I want you to have this," she said.

"Why, certainly," I said. And suddenly, the quilt was mine. It was sort of a mystery quilt, emerging from the chest that I had never looked inside. I wondered what else was in there, but I knew not to look. At the time, I did not value the deeper meaning of the quilt.

I was a wild child who did not preserve dolls or keep my tea party china intact. Somehow Betsy Wetsy's head ended up on Chatty Cathy's naked body, and their hair looked like an attack of the cooties.

But something about the quilt spoke to me, and it is only now that I understand the message. It whispered life and love and preservation and hope, all unfolded and passed down to me in hand-sewn stitches of love.

Our quilts will forever be a comfort on a cold rainy day in November, or in a heat wave in the middle of the night in August, for they are stitched with a thread that will endure through heat and cold, love and loss.

I like knowing that.

## Granny

I had the best granny in the whole wide world. When I wanted a new pet, she helped me smuggle a duck into my mother's car. She always listened when I talked, and I talked a lot. She let me meddle in her jewelry and listen in on the party line. On Friday nights, we ate popcorn and watched Alfred Hitchcock movies. Our favorite was *The Birds*.

Granny sang hymns while I helped in the kitchen. When she sang "The Old Rugged Cross," it felt like Jesus had been crucified right there in her back yard on the hill behind the cherry tree, out by the pond.

Of all the loved ones I have lost, I miss my granny the most. She would have been ninety-eight years old today.

Although she died in 1982, Granny breezed in early this morning and inspired me to write this poem. True to form, she gave me a present on her birthday.

My granny was like that.

"When Granny Said a Prayer for Me" is dedicated to all the good grannies in this world.

Your prayers are heard, and you do make a difference.

*When Granny Said a Prayer for Me*

Granny made my biscuits
Granny made my tea
Granny grated coconut
And said a prayer for me

Granny rocked me gently
While bullfrogs croaked at night.
When Granny said a prayer for me
The darkness turned to light

Granny sat beside me
Out on the old porch swing
And sprinkled sunshine on my soul
Whenever she would sing

Granny smelled like buttercups—
And apple pie and rain.
She was made of roses
And tulips and meringue

Granny was an angel
Recalled in '82
I sat alone in that old swing
And wondered what to do

Who would make my biscuits?
Who would pour my tea?
Who would grate my coconut
And say a prayer for me?

Now Granny comes to visit
I can feel her in the air
She sprinkles sunshine on my soul
Her love is everywhere

Don't ask me to explain it
For I don't understand
How Granny left in '82
Yet holds on to my hand

Why fret about tomorrow
Or toss and turn at night?
My Granny said a prayer for me
And everything's all right

Now when I grate the coconut
I feel her close to me
And she will watch the biscuits
While I go pour the tea

## I Like It Like That

As a child, I spent a lot of time in church. Three times a week, my family and I would tromp into the large downtown church building that stood tall and proud on the very downtown street on which I grew up, and we would sit in our respective places. My parents always sat in the same place—smack dab in the middle pew of the middle aisle. My father's parents always sat in the middle aisle on a front-row seat, and my mother's parents did not sit together.

My maternal grandfather always sat toward the front on the far left aisle, where the portable hearing aids were. Throughout his life, he maintained a certain childlike curiosity, a naivety that evoked innocence and awe. It was this very curiosity that made him want to hear what the preacher had to say, and I watched as he absorbed every word with no sign of judgment, boredom, scoffing, disdain, or envy.

My maternal grandmother sat in the same left aisle toward the back, with her friend "Miss Grace." Granny and Miss Grace had a cozy time in church—they were childhood friends who often snickered and giggled during the service, but they were never rude or distracting. The nearest they ever came to distraction was once when Granny yawned and a fly flew in her mouth. The sight of watching her discreetly swat the fly from her mouth while trying to appear godly and tactful was a sight to behold, and after the fly flew away, she and Miss Grace giggled so hard the pew shook.

It was this type of event that made church tolerable for me. Unlike my grandfather, I did not cling to the preacher's every word with any degree of awe. From an early age, it was my nature to question the words the preacher said, because they did not ring true in my mind. The roaring admonitions of sin from the pulpit, the banging of the fist on the podium, the wiping of a sweaty brow with a neatly pressed white handkerchief, seemed like a circus show to me.

I'd sit and envision the wife ironing the preacher's handkerchief while he was stretched out in his easy chair eating ice cream and then snoring the night away, and then I'd think about how much fun it would be to stand up there and scream at everybody and bang my fist on the wooden podium and make people writhe with guilt while extending the invitation and belting out "Almost Persuaded." I sometimes wondered, if given the chance, it might be possible for me to make them crawl down the aisle, crying out in sin and shame.

I never had a permanent seat in church because I liked to move around and check out the view from different angles. When I was young, I sat with my parents and grandparents, and when I got older I sat with my friends. Occasionally, I would take a break and move back to Granny and Miss Grace, and on rare occasions I would sit alone.

I recall one night in particular, a Sunday night in June, when I walked into church and plopped down on a pew in the middle aisle toward the back, all by myself. I was around twelve years old, right on the cusp of hormonal disarray. I checked both clocks—the one in the front to the right of the pulpit, and the one in back that the preacher could see—to make sure they were in sync. Right before the preaching began, a woman I'd known all my life leaned up from behind and said, "Why, Julie! Your hair is wet!"

I turned around and said, "I like it like that." The sermon ended and we went home and through the years the woman reminded me of the time she told me my hair was wet and how I replied, "I like it like that." It seemed to make an impression on her and in the back of my mind I wondered why. But I didn't wonder or care enough to give it much thought at the time.

Years have passed and things have changed. The downtown church in my hometown was torn down and replaced by a funeral home. Most of the "older" members in the congregation have died.

I still question the role of the preacher, and I still do not believe in screaming and pounding and manipulation through guilt.

I have wondered why the damp hair incident made such an impression on the woman behind me, who always sat in the same back pew in the middle aisle. Why did she bring up my reply, "I like it like that," throughout the years? To me, it was a mundane reply that did not register on my cerebral map. But to her it meant something else entirely: My own opinion of what I wanted at such a young age, along with my willingness to state it in blunt terms was unfathomable to her, and I think that is a sad thing.

Do I have regrets regarding my church beliefs and my damp hair and my lack of commitment to a permanent seat? No, I do not. I appreciate having grown up in a town and in a church where not only everybody knew my name, some cringed when they heard it and probably still do. I appreciate the voice inside that whispered it was acceptable to go to church with damp hair and to sit anywhere I wanted and to think creatively in order to endure the twisting of the truth.

That is the way it was and shall forever be, and I like it like that.

## The Southern Funeral

Yes, time travel exists. Last week I attended a funeral in my hometown and went back twenty years. I saw the people I grew up with, still looking the same, still glad to see me. At funerals, the past blurs and the familiarity of family and friends sucks you in like a drug and you feel safe and secure.

Robert Frost wrote, "Home is the place where, when you have to go there, they have to take you in."

Come, take my hand and travel with me through my hometown funeral parlor.

The room is decorated with red carnations and yellow daisies. There are a couple of fireside baskets, and there are peace lilies in each corner. To the right there is a large gardenia plant, loaded with sweet exotic blooms.

The casket is open and the corpse rests under the dim glow of the funeral lamp at either end of his eternal bed.

If he could talk back, he might utter these words:

- "Natural, my ass."
- "Cut the crap, Paw-Paw. You hated my guts and you know it."

- "Put that rose back!"
- "I'm dead—what's your excuse?"

Southern funerals are more than just a gathering place for politicians. They're great for catching up on local gossip. Be still and listen to the conversation:

"Look, there's Jane! They say she married an Episcopalian millionaire. Even has a summer cottage in Maine."

"Oh, he forgave Irene. He just refused to speak to her after she creamed him in court."

"I always heard Ray dressed up like a woman whenever Agnes went out of town."

The room is filled with old ladies sitting with their ankles crossed, dabbing at their eyes with handkerchiefs and holding onto their pocketbooks. They sit reminiscing about when their husbands died and wonder out loud who'll be next.

"I heard Ed's liver was plumb eat up with cancer."

"Oh Lord, what in the world will Cleo do without him?"

"Sister, she'll just have to get over it like the rest of us."

Back in the kitchen, unfinished business is frozen in time. The Styrofoam cups are half-filled with black coffee, the crowded ashtrays are overflowing with stubbed-out cigarettes, and the table is abandoned with half-eaten stale doughnuts and wadded-up napkins. The chairs are pulled out and empty.

Out in the hall, we see small children tugging at their mothers' hems and their fathers' coats. Inside the ladies room, we see fat women stuffed into their Sunday dresses, wrestling with their pantyhose and losing the war.

And now the service begins.

We have the stubby preacher wiping his brow and banging his fist on the podium, proclaiming salvation and what a good Christian man this drunkard was. By the time he gets through, everyone is wondering who he's talking about, and hoping the same lies will be spoken at their own funerals.

Now scoot closer and listen as a clear voice sings "Abide with Me." Watch as my tears fall from the words of the song and the sweetness of the memory.

The preacher closes with *Psalm 23*, and we turn on our headlights to enter the funeral procession. A policeman directs traffic with little effort, because in the South every trash of creation pulls off the road to honor the deceased.

There is a tent at the cemetery because it always rains at the burial. It is a Southern tradition. The preacher graciously bends over and extends his hand to the immediate family, making his way down the row of folding chairs and whispering soft words of comfort.

The tears fall with the rain while an A Capella quartet sings "Beulah Land." One more life on Earth is complete, and the body is lowered into the ground.

Walk with me up the steps to my ancestral home, where we gather in the living room and eat fried chicken, country ham and biscuits, pecan pie, and chocolate cake.

Sit down beside me while I thumb through old photos and chat with folks I won't see again until the next funeral. I only hope and pray it won't be my children's, my spouse's or my own.

The Southern funeral is a time machine that takes you home, if only for a moment.

Home is the place where, when you have to go there, they have to take you in.

Amen.

## The Ten Commandments

It is a known fact that our brains automatically reject negative wording. For example, if we say to ourselves, "Do not eat that doughnut," we will end up licking the box. And if we say to ourselves, "Do not smoke that cigarette," we will be on our second pack by the time *As the World Turns* goes off.

The question of whether the Ten Commandments should be displayed on public property is a hot topic in the moral realm of society. Some people believe that if only the words "Thou Shalt Not Commit Adultery" had been etched in the White House, Bill Clinton would have turned his head from Monica Lewinski, and there would be no stain on the blue Gap dress or analysis of the word "is."

If the Ten Commandments are to be displayed on public property, they should be reworded in positive terms so that our minds will automatically accept them. The Seventh Commandment, "Thou shalt not commit adultery" could read, "If you commit adultery you will be responsible for causing someone else to violate the Sixth Commandment, "Thou shall not kill," and you will also have to pay alimony, child support, and dry-cleaning expenses before you land in the pond otherwise known as Hell."

Here in the South, we seem to do pretty well with the first negative statement, "Thou shalt not make unto thee any graven image," so we'll leave that one alone. After all, if we don't know what it means, we ain't gonna do it.

But the second negatively stated commandment, "Thou shalt not take the name of the Lord thy God in vain; for the Lord will not hold him guiltless that taketh His name in vain," should be restated so that old-timey Southern women could take heed and be saved.

This particular commandment has always been a major concern of mine, because of my Great-Aunt Tut who invented the Baptist church. She often said, "Why, Lord, no!" And sometimes my grandmother would respond to human conditions such as fatigue or improper grammar with "Lordy, Lordy." Hopefully, they'll be cut some slack on this one.

Most of us are able to keep the sixth commandment, "Thou shalt not kill," but for deranged people like serial killers, this commandment should read "If you kill for pleasure, you will receive no media attention whatsoever, and your prison cell will be a replica of the lone Hell cell in which you will spend eternity."

Sadly, we struggle with commandments eight and nine, "Thou shalt not steal," and "Thou shalt not bear false witness against thy neighbor." This is a mystery, since the word "steal" is a simple one. However, the term "bear false witness" was not on any standardized testing while we were in school; therefore, it is probable that we commit this sin out of sheer ignorance. Simply stated, these commandments could read, "If you steal or lie, you will go to Hell."

The last negatively stated commandment is number ten, "Thou shalt not covet thy neighbor's house, thou shalt not covet thy neighbor's wife, nor his manservant, nor his maidservant, nor his ox, nor his ass, nor anything that is thy neighbor's."

The Tenth Commandment often leaves us with the question, "What can we do?" Therefore, it should be restated to read, "Move to the country and surround yourself with things you hate to look at and would never covet, such as dead horses and thistles, and turn your head from oxen, asses, or other people."

Lordy, Lordy, that Tenth Commandment's a pain in the ass.

## Death vs. Vacation Bible School

Let's face it, our biggest fear is death, unless our summer vacation has ended, and it is time to return to our worldly work on Earth, otherwise known as a job. Recently, I attended the funeral of a dear family friend who will be missed by many. This friend was my mother's best friend, and therefore, she shared a great sense of humor and a unique and healthy way of looking at life.

She was resilient and she will be missed, but like my mother she will live on because she bestowed genuine love upon so many, and love lives on forever, for there is no greater gift, with the exception of Vacation Bible School.

Since I have lived the most part of my life in the South, I have only attended Southern funerals and therefore have no desire to attend a funeral from any other part of the country, for these funerals appear to be sparse, superficial, disrespectful, and boring.

Granted, I have only viewed non-Southern funerals on TV, but somehow I sense they are the antithesis of the Southern funeral, the real deal which involves casserole ladies, pound cake ladies, fried chicken ladies, pecan pie ladies, ham-and-biscuit ladies, and other food ladies too numerous to mention.

Let's be honest here. At the Southern funeral, food reigns. Truth is, if there is no spread of food large enough to feed all the starving children in Ethiopia, the deceased did not amount to much. Add to that the counting of the flower arrangements, and an accurate assessment will be made.

In the case of my dear friend, she counted a whole lot, but in no way do I measure her merit by food or flowers. That pecan pie was spectacular, though.

As luck would have it, my friend's death occurred during the sacred week of Vacation Bible School. Before the children were even informed of their mother's death, the head-honcho church food lady called the house, asking when and where the food should be delivered.

My friend's daughter replied that she did not know because she was in the midst of making arrangements for the family's arrival, many of whom lived out of town.

The Food Queen went on to inquire about the specific date and time of the funeral, upon which the daughter replied, "I don't know. We just found out she was dead."

"Well, when do you THINK the funeral will be?" inquired the Food Queen.

Admirably, the daughter said, "Well, I don't know. Tentatively, I would say it will be Friday at eleven o'clock."

"We can't have that!" screamed the Food Queen. "We are having Vacation Bible School this week, and the preacher won't be able to be there!"

"You'll just have to check back with me on that," said the daughter, who tactfully hung up and proceeded to call her siblings.

Meanwhile, my friend's children made the funeral arrangements and rearranged their work schedules and such, for in reality, funerals do require a change of plans, especially in the case of a mother.

An hour later, Food Lady called the daughter back and said, "You cannot have the funeral on Friday at eleven. We are having Vacation Bible School this week and the preacher will not be able to attend the funeral. What do you want us to do with the food?"

And then my friend's daughter did what no daughter has ever done before. She said, "Look, my mother has died, and all I care about is paying her the proper respect from her children. We can order pizza or barbeque, and you can stick your food up your posterior."

But, of course, she did not use the word "posterior," and I just loved every minute of it.

The saga did not end there, however. At the moment of the final family viewing of the body, Food Queen appeared and said, "The food is going to get spoiled! What do you want us to do with it?"

Rest assured my friend's daughter had a curt reply.

Suffice it to say our dear friend had a nice funeral, complete with preacher, flowers, and an abundance of food.

And for her, that would have been more than plenty.

### Our Father Who Art in School

Forwarded e-mail tends to repeat itself, and I am amazed at the seemingly intelligent people who send messages full of propaganda. Yesterday, I received four e-mails regarding prayer in schools, urgently coaxing me to forward the message to everyone in my address book so that prayer could be reinstated in our public schools. As an added bonus, I would receive a free Old Navy gift card.

I'd like to know when the freedom to pray was removed. How is it possible to prevent someone from praying?

I taught for thirty years in public schools, and I witnessed ample prayer. Students pray to pass the test. Teachers pray for three o'clock. Principals pray for conferences in Gatlinburg.

Our poor children, I am told, are forbidden to pray in schools. And it is this absence of prayer in schools that has caused everything from school shootings to pinworms.

Back when we had prayer in schools, the grass was always green, the sky was always blue, and the sun was always shining.

Back when we had prayer in schools, classrooms were devoid of profanity, teachers felt safe, and Bayer aspirin was the only drug around. Were these trends absent because of public school prayer, or were they absent because parents disciplined their children at home? Back then, more parents were actually at home to manage their family lives.

It is crucial that we understand the cause-and-effect aspects of then and now. Some people would even suggest that back when we had prayer in schools, folks from different political and religious walks of life held hands and sang "Row, Row, Row Your Boat" on a daily basis.

And then they had to go mess up a good thing.

"It was the strangest thing," says Louise, an eighty-five-year-old geometry teacher at the high school. "The day they banned prayer in schools, a big pink wart popped out on my left elbow. Had a little smiley face right in the middle of it."

"My little Billy had never had a cavity until prayer was banned in school," says Martha Joyce. "A month later his front teeth rotted out, and he went into a full set of dentures by age seventeen."

By golly, let's just mosey on back to the good old days. Let's reinstate school prayer in public schools.

Picture this with one eye shut:

Prayer is reinstated and Ms. Chalkdust, the first-grade teacher, is kneeling before her class on her polar bear prayer rug. "Dear Lord," she says, "thank you for acknowledging my prayers. Thank you for allowing me to live in a country where I can live an openly gay lifestyle. Thank you for allowing me to preach as an ordained minister in my church. Thank you for allowing me to be pro-choice in my beliefs as a woman. Thank you for giving me the opportunity to influence these young minds in prayer and in accordance with your divine love and acceptance."

In walks Mr. Newsocks, the principal. He interrupts Ms. Chalkdust and says, "Whoa, there, Nelly. You just wait a minute, sister. You're not supposed to be leading a prayer. Why, you're a woman! And what's this 'openly gay lifestyle' hogwash? You can't be carrying on like that around here. It's blasphemous!"

"Why Mr. Newsocks, where have you been for the past thirty years? You can't discriminate against me on the basis of my sexual orientation or my religious beliefs. These children have a right to be exposed to free thinking and free religion. Don't you realize that's one of the benefits of the reinstatement of public prayer? Isn't this what you wanted? After all, you were the biggest advocate in the county for school prayer. Be careful what you wish for, Mr. Newsocks. Be very careful."

Prayer still runs rampant in our public schools, and it will as long as people want it to. Oh, the words may not be fancy and loud, and they may not be read from an index card, but God still hears them.

I'm told He prefers silent prayers anyway.

## Coffee with God

January flew by and washed our New Year's resolutions out in the flood.

Now, February brings us valentines, Martin Luther King, and a sprinkling of snow. Looks like God took a giant salt shaker and said, "Aw, what the heck. They have plenty of snow days."

Thank you, God. The snow was no coincidence. I talk to God most mornings, and I begged Him for that stuff.

There is an art in talking to God. Two years ago, a self-help junkie friend of mine gave me one of those hokey self-affirmation calendars. On January 22, it said clarity increased your chances of getting your prayers answered, so I decided to give it a shot. Now, I get very specific when I'm tuning in with God. I tell Him my name, my address, the time, and the date. Also, I've found that God wants me to be comfortable when talking to Him, so I keep my eyes open and I drink my first cup of coffee during our sunrise chat.

There's nothing better than coffee with God.

When I was a little girl, I prayed and prayed for a trampoline. I just knew one morning I would wake up and there it would be, gleaming in my back yard, waiting for me to bounce up and down on it and break my neck. The trampoline never came, so I continued to jump on my bed and turn flips.

I suspect Mama had been talking to God.

In my adult life, I used to pray for other material things. Bigger house, loving nanny, huge publishing deal, that sort of thing. Never happened, or at least it hasn't yet.

But after I started having coffee with God, things changed. Oh, I'm still in the same packed house, and I'm still the only nanny in sight. The publishing deal is still a hope and a prayer, but it is not a top concern. Now, my top concern is to recognize when my prayers have been answered. My prayers go something like this:

"God, this is Julie on February 9, 2011. It's 5:03 a.m.

Thank you for the coffee, God, and thank you for keeping everyone else asleep so I can talk to you in stillness and peace. Thank you for my family's health, and thank you for all that you have given us.

Today I ask that you help me to remain focused enough to do half the things on my to-do list. I beg you to keep me from screaming at my husband and kids. Keep my mind clear and free from anger, and help me to be a good influence on others.

Most of all, God, continue to show me the truth. There is nothing more powerful.

And thanks again for the coffee, God.

Amen."

Not a very elaborate prayer, I know, but on the days I forget to have coffee with God, I notice I'm not as productive and my mood isn't as light.

"Do you really believe you have to be that specific when you pray?" asks my husband. "After all, it's God you're talking to. He knows everything. He even knows what you want before you put in your request. Why bother?"

I bother because I believe God likes for me to ask. Oh, He may still be around when I forget to call, but He likes to hear His name. Sure, He can read my mind and He knows all my secrets, but He still likes the sound of my voice.

Kind of like wanting to hear the words "I love you," whispered into your ear from your true love.

God likes thankfulness and acknowledgment, and He likes good manners. If you don't believe me, try it sometime.

And remember to say thanks.

## Milk Carton Religion

Do you remember when we were kids, and the back of the red and white milk carton pictured a church with a steeple, along with the words "Attend your church regularly"?

I always figured that since it was on the milk carton, attending church was not an option. After years of eating my cereal and staring at the back of the milk carton in a Froot Loop trance, I read the words out loud to my mother: "Attend your church regularity."

She let out one of her famous maniacal laughs, lit up a cig, and called up her two best friends to let them know that I had mispronounced the word "regularly" and called it "regularity," as in Ex-Lax. There was nothing in this world that tickled my mother more than a mispronounced word, except when somebody fell down the steps and went splat on the ground or in the grass.

Ah, those were the days when assumptions could be made, such as the need for everyone to attend church regularly. In today's world, the milk company would be sued for violation of The First Amendment if they prompted us to attend church. In today's world, if we still had pictures on the backs of milk cartons, we might see an emaciated cat with a caption that read "Save the cow. Drink soy milk."

Luckily the South has not changed a whole lot, and many of us still attend church regularly. I have to wonder if it was the subliminal message on the milk carton that became permanently embedded in our young minds. Whatever the case, I'm glad we still attend church regularly, and I'm even more thankful that we have a choice. That choice does not mean we have to agree, however. I'm also thankful for the disagreement, because this world would be a boring place if we all agreed on religion, that sensitive little topic.

Lately, we have had religious bickering here in our hometown, and I have to ask: Where is Church Lady when you need her? It seems the "God loves me but He's worried about you" mentality is running amok here. It seems that even those who have been attending church with regularity have ended up in the hot seat. This means people who have been sleeping, fishing, and golfing on Sundays have somehow gotten away with irregularity.

Some might say, "That ain't right," and I would agree. After all, these people followed the instructions on the milk carton. After all, they got out of bed and put on their Sunday clothes instead of picking up a fishing pole or a golf club. They may be in the hot seat down here, but I'll bet they're getting Brownie points up there somewhere.

Maybe some of us need to take a chill pill and admit that our interpretation of the Bible is not the one and only. Maybe we need to put down the Bible for a day or two and go out and help a homeless person or an emaciated cat. Maybe we need to sleep in, or go fishing or golfing, but not on a Sunday. I read it on the milk carton.

My mother attended church regularly, but I'll bet she got some points taken off when she made fun of linguistic mishaps and staircase tumbles. As in life, there are admonitions in the Bible that are more important than others. The Bible tells us that God knows all of our secrets, and that's my main focus.

If it were up to me I'd even put it on the milk carton.

## The One That Got Away

My sister and I recently attended the funeral of a hometown friend who was born into a family of men who have managed to convince themselves and others that they are the only people going to Heaven, because everyone else is WRONG.

Yes, the place was packed with uncles, brothers-in-law, and cousins, espousing Scripture and whispering about the will. They call themselves gospel preachers, but I prefer the term "sheep in black."

At many Southern funerals, a blanket of familiarity comforts those left behind. We go home and see all the old familiar faces and places and manage to forget why we ever moved away in the first place.

But at this particular funeral, the blanket of familiarity was of no comfort. At every turn was a gospel preacher, standing guard like a gunman outside a Mexican bank, and I never even noticed the flowers because I was constantly on the lookout for my male captors—the preachers who knew me from my escaped past. They might call me the sheep in black, but I prefer "the one that got away."

Now, don't get me wrong. I am not referring to *all* preachers here, or even *most* preachers. I am referring to the ones who've managed to reach a smug, elitist pinnacle in life, from which they look down and see entire oceans of black sheep, except when they look in the mirror. Luckily, their numbers are few, because insanity will do that to a leader and his flock.

The casket was closed. The sons, handsome young men, watched their father lie in state with yellow tulips atop his chest.

I whispered to my sister, "I'll be right back if I ever get out of here," and I went to the ladies room and thought about Mama. At funerals, she always said two things: "He looks so natural," and "Death is such a final thing."

With the biggest of duhs, my sisters and I would march down the aisle with her and stare at the corpse, praying that just this once, she would keep her mouth shut.

The funeral began and my grief quickly turned to anger at the words that were both spoken and unspoken by the preachers. By the time they sang "Peace in the Valley," I was ready to belt someone, and I remembered why I left this town in the first place.

The dead cannot speak for themselves, and a funeral is not the place to point out deficiencies. Here, there were no highlights of a life well-lived or memories of goodness and reassurance of grace. Instead, there were references to the term "gutter drunk" and mentions of judgment, eternity, and HELL.

They sang "Softly and Tenderly," but the manipulation in the air interfered, and the words and the melody failed to stir my heart. The damage had been done, and I thought to myself, Something is wrong with this picture—only a heathen could botch "Softly and Tenderly."

I almost went down there to speak up for our old friend. Who would have stopped me? Not only would it have fulfilled my dream of dressing up like Tina Turner and rocking down the sacred aisle, it would have set a precedent for women to speak up at Southern funerals. After all, we gave birth to these male pontificates. Verily.

I will miss my old friend. But I will take comfort in knowing that somewhere, there is peace in the valley, and that he is there, at rest.

## Inevitability of Miracles

*"Without knowing it, he followed the same self-route the doctor had taken some eight months earlier, and in a world of infinite possibilities where all journeys share a common end, perhaps they are together, taking the evening air on a ruined veranda among the hollyhocks and oleanders, the doctor sipping his scotch and the paperhanger his San Miguel, gentlemen of leisure discussing the vagaries of life and pondering deep into the night not just the possibility but the inevitability of miracles."*

—William Gay, excerpt from *"The Paperhanger"*

My friend William Gay died last week, and I will miss him, as will all of his friends and massive fans. Back in March 2004, I interviewed William Gay, critically acclaimed writer, and the interview was published in *The Daily Herald* on March 7, 2004.

There have been two times in my life that I have sensed inevitability: The first time was when I was a senior in high school, and that one did not turn out well. Still, there was that sense of inevitability, that sense that something was about to happen over which I had no control.

The second time I experienced the sense of inevitability was in late October 2002, when William Gay and his son Chris Gay were to perform on the "Thacker Mountain" radio show in Oxford, Mississippi. I was headed down to Oxford to visit our daughter Katy that weekend, and I knew that somehow, I would run into William Gay, although I would not seek him out, because it seemed inevitable, meaning that there was nothing I had to do.

My interest in William Gay originated from a reference he made to my great-grandfather, "Pappy Rasbury," in William's first published book, *The Long Home*. I will add that my connection to the Rasburys was strong and protective and sweet and somewhat clannish, and I knew somehow that we would cross paths, because I knew that somehow, he was like the Wayne County Rasburys and that was a sweet and pure thing. It is my belief that people who grow up in this neck of the woods need to stay close to home.

Sure enough, as I was walking down the stairs at Square Books on a Sunday morning in Oxford, on November 2, 2002, at 10:30 a.m., there he was, with a perky young woman by his side. And it just so happened that I had just purchased his new collection of short stories, *I Hate to See That Evening Sun Go Down.*

I walked over to him and asked, "Are you William Gay?"

"I think so," he said, and seeing his book that was clutched firmly to my heart, he asked, "You want me to sign your book?"

"No," I said. "You've already signed it." And then I made mention of Pappy Rasbury, and we talked about our local connection.

Meanwhile, the young girl lit up and said, "We want William to move to Oxford! We just love him down here!"

I said, "William's not going anywhere but Hohenwald. That's the only place he can write." And then I realized that my adrenaline level had risen, and that I was not competing in a basketball game with Loretto, Tennessee, anymore, and I calmed myself down without knocking her into the bleachers or fouling out.

Over the years, William Gay and I continued to talk, at first about writing and music, and then to more local concerns such as the behavior of our children and the rising cost of coffee and beans. While I admire and appreciate William's rare talent that is compared to William Faulkner, Flannery O'Connor, and Cormac McCarthy, it is the local, normal conversations that I will cherish the most.

William Gay and I each have four children: Two girls and two boys, all grown. In our later conversations, we spoke mostly about our children, and it was clear to me that his children were his top priority. He was not remotely interested in reading reviews about his writing, and he enjoyed his privacy, which I respected.

William occasionally got a kick out of things I would say to him. Back to the Rasbury connection, I told him that my beloved Rasbury grandmother had a bookshelf in her living room that contained a minimal portion of books that I had loved to look at since my childhood. One of the books was titled *Naked Came I* by David Weiss. I told William that throughout my life, I dared not touch that book because my visual perception of the title was sinful, in that it appeared to read "Naked Camei."

I always wondered: Why was Camei naked? Surely this was not a book that I was supposed to touch, much less open, because Camei was naked! William laughed at my perception and said it was a highly significant book.

I will add that William knew details about every book I ever mentioned to him, because he spent much of his life reading and studying the patterns of the writing therein.

One day I mentioned to William that back in high school, I had read Jacqueline Susann's book, *Once is Not Enough*, and he said, "That is the stupidest book ever written."

But we laughed, and I was not offended. After all, I read it in a beauty shop, and it was quite shocking to me at such a tender and vulnerable age.

My friend William Gay won both the James A. Michener Memorial Prize and the William Peden Award, and he received a Guggenheim Fellowship. In addition, he was named a 2007 USA Ford Foundation Fellow and awarded a $50,000 grant by United States Artists, a charity that supports and promotes the work of American artists.

William, I will miss you always, and so will the rest of your friends, family, and fans. You will live on through your writing, and I find comfort in that belief. Although you are gone from this harsh world in which you wrote about, we will take care of you and your precious children.

Press on, William. Press on.

# GERITOL MOMENTS

## Moans and Groans

There are differences between the first year of marriage and the eighteenth year.

The first year it's moans, and the eighteenth year it's groans. Yes, by the eighteenth year, the love nest has been blown out of the tree, and there are other areas of focus. What to eat for supper, for example, and which antacid to take afterward. Watching your teenagers toss all your money into a bottomless pit, knowing it will only get worse in college.

The thrill ride of the first year becomes a bumper car moment by the eighteenth, but there are advantages. You are older, wiser, and proud to be alive. By the eighteenth year, you have either decided there is nothing to appreciate, or you have begun to appreciate the simpler things in life, such as a walk on the beach or a warm snuggle on a cold dark night.

The first year of marriage, there was no night, because we did not sleep. As a result, babies soon followed, and we began to crave sleep. Isn't it ironic?

Now in our eighteenth year of marriage, the sleepless nights have returned, but it's different somehow. Just the other night, I was awakened by the sound of my husband burping into my right ear. "You just burped in my ear," I said.

"I know," he replied. "I can do it even louder with my mouth open."

Laughter followed, and soon we found ourselves in the midst of a burping contest at two in the morning. I won.

Next, we did a comparison study of the original Pepcid AC versus the new Pepcid AC that can be sucked on, like a Tums. He prefers the original, even though the new one contains the same active ingredients. I like the new stuff.

In the eighteenth year of marriage, "Oh yeah, baby" means he's agreed to get the paper and make the coffee.

Pajamas have changed dramatically by the eighteenth year. The first year it was all those slinky, sexy, spaghetti strap teddy things that became twisted and gnarled in the night. Now it's sweat suits and soccer socks. I do try to vary the color of my socks, but the sweats are always gray. I am especially fond of the purple soccer socks, but lately I have been wearing the red ones because Valentine's Day is drawing near.

Now, I look forward to chocolates on Valentine's Day. In our first year of marriage, he sent me a dozen red roses at work. All the women snickered and said, "Better get a long whiff of 'em, honey, because this is the last time he'll ever do this."

How did they know?

Anyway, my husband tolerates the soccer socks, but he hates the sweats. When warm weather rolls around, I'll dig out the slinky stuff and slip into something a little less comfortable.

During the first year of marriage, everything was sparkling and new. Smiles sparkled with innocence and ecstasy, and furniture sparkled because there were no children. By the eighteenth year, the teeth have begun to fade, and the furniture has either been replaced or is in dire need. The innocence is gone, but in a good marriage, the ecstasy will remain. It may not be as frequent, because it is hard to be exhausted and ecstatic at the same time.

Have you ever craved what you couldn't have, just when you thought you needed it most? Of course you have, because that is the nature of life. The only exception to this is that first year of marriage, when you might very well think you have everything you ever thought you needed, because you are hopelessly, totally, wildly in love. By the eighteenth year, family issues have surfaced and reared their ugly heads, and one way or another, you have learned to deal with it.

Passion is no substitute for experience. But it sure comes close.

## Insomnia

I don't sleep well. Sometimes it's the cats, sometimes it's the wind, sometimes it's a nightmare. The other night my husband was also struck by insomnia, and everything hit all at once: the cats were leaping on top of us like kangaroos, I had a nightmare, and the wind was howling, while my husband tossed and turned. I decided to go to the couch.

"Where are you going?" he asked.

"To the couch," I said. "You're flopping around like a dolphin on dry land, and I can't sleep."

But for some reason, I stayed in bed and never made it to the couch. We ended up talking about our favorite childhood TV shows, such as *My Friend Flicka*, *Flipper*, and *My Three Sons*. We talked about how his family liked *Bonanza* and how my grandmother liked *Hogan's Heroes*, and we talked about Misty, our thirteen-year-old cat that plots against us and keeps us up at night.

Many times, we have considered taking Misty to the animal shelter because she has no redeeming qualities, but in the end, we just can't do it. She is our pet, and our children like to hold her. The other day she was sitting quietly in our youngest child's lap, and he said, "I think Misty is going to live forever. Don't ever take her to the animal shelter."

"She couldn't catch a bird with two broken wings," said his brother. "She's stupid, but I like her, too."

And so it's settled. Misty will grow old with us while we lie awake at night and reminisce about old black-and-white TV shows and worry about our kids and our lives.

It's useless to worry, but the mind can be an illogical thing, and worries will peak in the dark of night when the only sounds are creaking floors and leaping cats and howling wind.

Insomnia struck us both again last night, this time simultaneously. "What are you thinking about?" my husband asked.

"Today is my parents' fifty-fourth wedding anniversary, but since Mama died eighteen years ago, they are no longer married," I said. "What are you thinking about?"

"A bunch of stuff," he said. "Work, the kids, school, and you."

"Why don't we just sell everything and walk down the beach for the rest of our lives?" I asked.

"We can't do that yet," he said. "We're too young, the kids are too young, and besides, cats don't like sand."

Promises, promises. My husband always keeps his promises, and that's good. Children take note of such things, and this will make a difference in their lives. But still it's tempting—the notion of chunking it all and walking down the beach for the rest of our lives, even though the logical part of my mind tells me whatever we're walking away from will tap us on the back with a big grin—wrinkles, age spots, sickness, death, and old cats. Waiting for test results, becoming grandparents, high cholesterol, heart disease, and cancer. These things may happen, but it's useless to worry.

From here on out, I'm going to remember the good times and replace my worried mind with happy thoughts, such as old friends, warm oatmeal cookies, red and yellow tulips, and my old upright piano, waiting for songs to be written and played while there's still time.

Now that's something to sleep on.

## Cat Naps

*"What was is was; what's done is done."*

— Julie Gillen

Now that I am retired, I am free to be my truly obnoxious self, so get ready.

It's an adjustment, a different world, after working outside the home after all these years since my first job at the age of fifteen, back when I "operated" the concession stand at the Lawrenceburg Golf and Country Club. Man, that was a hard job, hanging out with my friends at the pool and popping an occasional pre-packaged hamburger into the microwave, back in the early '70s when microwaves cost three thousand bucks.

I'm older now, as in hormonal. And I'm not talking about the type of hormonal that inhabited my body at age fifteen—it's a whole new ballgame at age fifty-three. But don't get me wrong, because I have found the perfect doctor for hormonal disarray, and I am thankful for that. The problem is, sometimes I run out of medication, and I have to call my doctor to inquire about certain concerns.

Two days ago I called him and left a message that said, "I ran out of fish oil pills so I swallowed a couple of my son's guppies. Is that okay?"

I have not heard back from him yet, and I'm feeling okay, so I'm assuming all is well on that front.

Sometimes I am invited out to lunch, now that I am retired, and recently a friend asked me the question of all female questions: "What are you going to wear?"

"Just wear what you wore yesterday," was my reply. I'm simple like that, which leads me into my next phase of retirement adjustment, related to both my clothing attire and my husband.

Recently he asked, "Just WHEN are you going to stop wearing your Scottie Dog pajamas and how many pairs of them do you own anyway?"

I told him I would wear them until the weather warmed up, and that I truly did not see what the problem was. He seemed to be okay with that, and later that morning I called him to ask what he wanted for lunch, which is also a whole new ballgame for me, but one that I heartily embrace.

I asked, "What do you want for lunch?"

He replied, "I won't be home for lunch, and I won't be home for supper."

"Long as you come home sometime that's all I care about," I said. "What are you doing for lunch?"

"I'm having lunch with Penny Lane," he said.

"What does she look like?" I asked.

"She's the coordinator for Ducks and Kittens, Inc.," he said.

"What does she LOOK like?" I asked.

"She's been doing this for fourteen years," he said.

"What does she LOOK like?" I asked again.

He paused. "I don't know. Somewhere between plain and okay, I guess."

Satisfied with his response, I said, "Well, you just be good, and I'll see you tonight, and we'll have a nice romantic dinner, minus the Scottie Dog pajamas."

"I look forward to that," he said.

Meanwhile, the muse hit and banged out a particle of a poem against my will. Disclaimer: The muse was *not* referring to my husband of twenty-nine years, to whom I am truly and thankfully devoted and in love with more than ever. Truth is, I was thinking about a certain evil female when the muse struck and screamed out …

*And if I die before I wake*
*I hope you meet a rattlesnake*
*And it will search inside your heart*
*And seeing nothing, will depart.*

Feeling rather pleased with my progress of the day thus far, I cozied up underneath my grandmother's quilt on our bed and decided to take a nap, feeling that after all those years, I deserved it. As luck would have it, our two cats had occupied the entire bed and gave me a look that said, "You're not going to make us move, are you?"

The muse reappeared as it sometimes does and presented me with yet another snippet of a poem titled "Housecat in Winter," which I will finish at some future point. Meanwhile, I did not make them move—I just scooted them over a bit, and the three of us took a delightful long winter's cat nap.

This is the story of my retirement thus far, and hopefully, it will be continued, complete with my husband, our cats, friends, and long winter's naps.

## With This Roast I Thee Wed

What is love?

Hell if I know.

Some people measure love by money. Other people measure love by diamonds. My husband measures love by a side of beef.

Like many married couples, my husband and I sometimes engage in mindless battles. We particularly like to argue over whose parents have demonstrated the most love. His parents always win hands down, because they have supplied us with beef for several years.

My parents merely supplied us with the ability to argue about any conceivable issue. Who's to say which is better?

If I knew then what I know now, I would have re-written my husband's wedding vows:

I now take you to be my lawfully wedded wife, in sickness and in beef, for T-bones for liver, for beefier for beefless, till cholesterol do us part. With this roast, I thee wed.

My mother measured love by a fresh pot of coffee, a carton of cigarettes, and other immediate gratification items. When I was in need, she gave me Barbie dolls, strawberry ice-cream cones, and Lifesavers.

I now know that while both sides of the family were lacking in the psychological ideal, mine fared worse. My wedding vows could have gone something like this:

"I now take you to be my lawfully wedded husband, in sickness and in addiction to sickness, for double-dipped and for coneless, for Folgers and for Maxwell House, till lung cancer do us part."

Love—I've spent a lifetime trying to understand it. What is love?

If it feels bad, is it really love? And if it feels good, is it always love? Am I in love with fried okra?

When I think of the word "love," several things pop into my head. I think of my life before marriage and my grandparents' farm with the huge maple tree out front. I think of climbing in that maple tree and hanging upside-down with my cousin, and making hand-cranked homemade ice cream underneath that maple tree on the Fourth of July. I think of backyard cookouts and birthday celebrations, and ice cream cones from the drugstore after church on Wednesday night. I think of knowing everybody in town, and liking them just because I'd known them all my life, and knowing they felt the same way about me.

I think of my husband, and I smile at the innocence and hope that existed in our early marriage. I think of the births of each of our children and re-live the magic.

Perhaps love is the innocence and the hope and the magic that sustains us all.

Perhaps love is simply doing the best you can, when you don't really know what you're doing.

I've been lucky to have a lot of love in my life. Without it, those T-bones wouldn't have tasted nearly as good and that strawberry ice cream wouldn't have made me smile. The maple tree wouldn't have held endless possibilities and the hometown wouldn't have wrapped me up and tucked me in like a huge security blanket.

And the coffee and cigarettes weren't bad, either.

## To Habit and to Hold

Through the years, I've quietly observed how friends and acquaintances cope with their spouse's bad habits. Mark Twain wrote, "Nothing so needs reforming as other people's habits."

It appears tolerance levels vary as much as people do. My friend Beth is married to Ralph, a smart and rich man. He's even witty at times. Problem is, Ralph's long toenails make her wince, but she doesn't have the nerve to tell him.

On the other hand, Jethro grows his toenails out intentionally, and Jolene finds them adorable.

Beth is further annoyed by Ralph's know-it-all commands behind the wheel. Phrases such as "Turn it tight!" "Ten-two position!" and "Look out for that mall!" make her cringe.

But when Jethro grabs the steering wheel and says, "Hold on baby—we're going for a ride," Jolene lights up a Marlboro, throws back her hair, and rolls down the window. Oh, how she loves her wild man.

Beth spends three hours in the bathroom and comes out looking like the bride of Bozo.

For her, "slipping into a pair of jeans" means flying to the Mall of America, trying on five thousand pairs, and involving Ralph in all aspects of her anguish along the way.

Ralph resents this.

Jolene, however, can grab a pair of jeans, shake her long blond head for a couple of seconds, swipe her lips with something shiny, and look like a million bucks.

Jethro appreciates this.

Psychologists say that in all fairness, habits that existed before the marriage may be irrevocable, but habits acquired after the marriage are open to pursuit, change, and even attack.

I asked Jolene what Jethro was like during their engagement period, and her reply was stunning.

"Oh, Jethro and I never really dated. We just had sex one night and decided to get married."

The union has worked. Jolene and Jethro have been married twenty-five years, but due to female problems, they have no children.

"I had one them uvarian sisks," says Jolene. "Big as a bowling ball. I told 'em just to rip out the whole thing. Be less for me to haul around."

Jethro agrees. "Aw, I'd kind of like a few younguns' running around here, but I figure Jolene's got all she can handle, keeping my butt in gear."

Jolene smiles and squeezes Jethro's hand. "The good Lord knew what he was doing when he put that sisk in me."

Beth's list of no-no's goes beyond toenails and driving orders. She also shuns teeth picking, ear digging, and nostril exploration.

But in Jethro's book, these are prerequisites for marriage. No-no's for some may be Brownie points for others. Jethro wears a catfish pendant around his neck. For their twentieth wedding anniversary, Jethro gave Jolene a catfish keychain engraved with the words "Nothing smells like a catfish."

People are different. If Jethro gave Beth a catfish, she'd get down on the floor and lick the toenails Ralph walked on. If Ralph gave barking orders to Jolene, she'd flare her nostrils, utter two simple words, and leap from the car.

Psychologists also say we should be sure the array of personality traits we find so adorable in the beginning will fit in with all of our future quirks.

For example, Jolene should ask herself these questions: Is Jethro's ability to burp "The Star Spangled Banner" a sign of true talent? Is his erotic-zone catfish tattoo really that cute? As Benjamin Franklin observed, "Your net worth to the world is usually determined by what remains after your bad habits are subtracted from your good ones."

Take note, Jolene: Do not use this equation on Jethro, unless you want him to disappear.

And as for Ralph, he disappeared a long time ago, shortly after Beth poofed from the scene.

And Jolene? A woman of rare form and class, she knows exactly who she is and what she wants. Jolene will be around for a long, long while.

## Sockies

*There was an old woman who lived in a shoe,*
*She had so many children, she didn't know what to do;*
*She gave them some broth without any bread,*
*She whipped them all soundly, and put them to bed.*

—Mother Goose

If that old woman were alive today, she'd be in Brushy Mountain for life for starving and whipping her children and living inside that ghetto shoe of hers.

Although my husband and I did not starve or whip our children, we also had so many children we didn't know what to do, and we still don't. If only there really were a big shoe to hide out in. Perhaps a heel or a toe or even a large shoelace in which to temporarily escape the responsibilities of parenthood.

One effect of having so many babies is that we use baby talk a lot without realizing it, even though most of our children are now grown and gone.

Just today as I was getting ready for work, my husband said, "Aren't you going to wear any sockies?"

"No, I can't find any sockies," I said. "Besides, no one's going to be looking at my ankles anyway, and if they ask, I'll just tell them this is what I do, like Don Johnson on *Miami Vice*."

"Well, what are they going to be looking at?" he asked. "Your NOSTRILS?"

"Yes," I said. "People have always admired my nostrils."

What my husband doesn't know is that I will grab a pair of his sockies on my way out, and he will never suspect a thing, because he doesn't read my column every single week, especially if I burn the paper.

When I got home from work, I tossed his sockies in the washing machine and flew up the stairs in naked ankles.

He was sitting on the couch. "Did anyone notice you weren't wearing any sockies?" he asked.

"No," I said. "And no one commented on my nostrils, either. Guess they're losing their shape." And then in an unprecedented move I said, "You know, hublet, I'm getting really tired of talking about ME."

"Oh, really?" he said. "Since WHEN? These days all you do is sing to the tune of 'Beethoven's Fifth Symphony': MEMEMEME! MEMEMEME! ME MEMEME, ME ME, ME ME, ME ME, ME MEMEMEEEEEE!"

And then I pushed my husband off the deck. That was two days ago, and he's still out there in a pile of leaves. I'll take him some broth and bread in a little while, but if I whipped him all soundly, he'd kick me out of the shoe, and I wouldn't blame him a bit. I did toss him a blankie the first night, and honestly, I think he's happy out there.

This is a great chance for me to steal more of his sockies, for it is supposed to rain soon, and he'll come back inside, wanting a cup of milkie and a bowl of homemade soupie.

I'm not sure, but I think it's possible for us to live happily ever after in this big old shoe of ours.

## Time

Who knows where the time goes? I only know that as we get older, time seems to fly by more quickly, and then we wake up one day and realize we are the same age our parents were when we got married.

They seemed so old! How can this be? I get out old photo albums and scrutinize our parents, and in truth, they did look older than we do now. But keep in mind that was back in the days before teeth whitening, cigarette warnings, and personal body trainers. Also, our parents did more manual labor back then than we do now, and their legitimate worries about money and the opinions of others contributed to their premature wrinkles.

Sometimes I think our parents were better off than we are today. They were raised in the pre-technology conformist era, and their roles were clearly defined. As with all compensation aspects of life, there was a price to pay, but still, the '50s generation had an innocence that no longer exists. I don't know if that's good or bad, but I know it is true.

Times have changed. Today the family farm is virtually nonexistent, and video games and computers have replaced public swimming pools and bicycles. Kids sleep till noon and play video games all afternoon, while both parents, who are often divorced, are hard at work in separate cities.

Somehow I am reminded of a song sung by the beautiful Jearlyn Steele, who often makes a guest appearance on Garrison Keillor's *A Prairie Home Companion* on Saturday night radio. The lyrics haunt me, and they asked a question something like this: If days are short and nights are long, why do we work so hard to get what we don't even want?

It is a very good question. Why do we work so hard to get what we don't even want?

When I was a kid, few of my friends' mothers worked outside the home. In the good old summertime, my own mother did not even see me until suppertime, and it was a win-win situation because she got to watch *As the World Turns* in peace, and I got to spend my days on my bicycle, riding over to friends' houses, but mostly swimming in the city pool where I had a season ticket.

At the peak of my high school years, my friends and I alternated between the Olympic-sized state park swimming pool and the country club pool, but the point is, I was never planted at home in front of the TV and neither was anyone else. We were out having fun in the sun, back in the pre-sunscreen era.

The whole thing makes me quite nostalgic. There are just some things that stick in your brain, such as the day President Kennedy was shot, and the day Elvis died.

I was at the country club pool in August 1977, sitting beside the lifeguard chair and listening to the radio when they interrupted "Free Bird" to announce that Elvis was dead. My brother-in-law, who was and still is eight years older than I am, screamed like a banshee.

I was nineteen years old, and yes, I was shocked to learn that Elvis was dead. But at the time, I viewed Elvis as a fat has-been in a white polyester jumpsuit singing Frank Sinatra songs. Frankly, I wanted to hear the end of "Free Bird."

That's the way it is when you are young. Somehow, I think it's all part of the plan.

## Cicada

Back in April 1985 when I was pregnant with our second baby, we moved back to Middle Tennessee with our first baby. Upon our arrival we immediately noticed a constant outdoor monotonous chirping sound that made it impossible to carry on a normal conversation in the outdoors. "What do you want for supper?" I would scream at my husband.

"I don't care!" he would scream back. "Just fix something quiet!"

We got settled in, and as is often the case in life, the fantasy did not match the reality. It was our first encounter with this type of experience, this inevitable moment of the end-of-an-era phase of the brief Barbie and Ken phase of the marital union. Like the cicadas that had been buried in the deep dark ground for thirteen years, we had suddenly emerged from our husked shells and we were in a new and unfamiliar place. It was hot, it was loud, and it was not romantic. It was the year of the cicada.

But nature, while unpredictable, is often kind. The cicadas disappeared in mid-June, our second baby girl was born in late September, and life was good.

By the summer of 1998, thirteen years later, we had four children, two cats, a mortgage, and a minivan. I also had a full-time job and a cell phone the size of a shoe box. One day in early June I was cruising up I-65 North in my minivan on my way to a school conference, listening to "I Don't Want to Wait" by Paula Cole, when the shoe box rang and all four kids were screaming.

"What's the matter with y'all?" I yelled.

"The cicadas are coming down the chimney, and the cats are eating them!" the oldest child, now a teenager, screamed, over the loud chirping sound of the cicada home invasion.

"Call your father!" I screamed, while trying to wave a cicada out of the van. "And close the damper in the fireplace!"

"What's the damper?" she screamed.

"It's that thing that keeps water and birds and cicadas from falling down the chimney. Your daddy will take care of it. Call him right now!"

I hung up, somehow confident that the cicadas would soon exit the house, and sure enough, they did. That was the last I recall of Cicada 1998.

Here we are, thirteen years later. Where did the time go? The children grew up and left home, I traded the minivan for a Volkswagen Beetle, and my iPhone fits inside my purse. Our oldest child now has a baby of her own, and lately she has been alarmed about the return of the cicada, one of her few fears.

The unseasonably cold spring weather has held the cicadas at bay so far, but they are out there and we know it. We see them on our trees and in our driveways and on our cars, and a few of them have managed to get into our houses. The best is yet to come, when the temperatures rise and the air will be filled with a deafening, high-pitched shrill as the males sound their mating call. It is the only chance they will ever get. Do I feel sorry for them? Of course not.

But I confess, I like the thirteen-year cicadas. There is something nostalgic about the predictability of their emergence from the ground and the way it reminds us of cicada years gone by. The cicadas represent milestones in our lives, and if we're lucky, we'll still be around in thirteen years to complain about the next brood.

Definitely something to wish for.

## Crunchy Ear

It's mid-June, and the family vacation has already come and gone, and I am thankful that everyone arrived and returned intact. It was a good vacation with no major mishaps, other than the sunburn on my lips and right ear. Turns out, Hubby also forgot to put sunscreen on his lips, and when he kissed me goodbye on his way to the golf course, we both screamed like we had just kissed a Tiki torch, or seen a positive pregnancy test.

I made a mental note that after twenty years of vacationing at the beach, our lips had never been sunburned, and I stuck it into the Twilight Zone portion of the scrapbook of our lives.

Now that the kids are older, I've noticed that vacations include not only fun and frolic, but also a poignant moment here and there, like the night I sat out on the deck in the dark, listening to the waves and peeping though the window at all of our grown children, like an invisible spectator. There was something comforting about being removed and yet so close, watching them all talk and laugh with each other. There was a realization that my babies were all grown up and that they were functioning well without me. Did this jab me in the heart like a maternal dagger from Hades? No.

It reminded me of a quote my brother-in-law used to say: "Once they all learn how to cut their own meat, it's all uphill." Another advantage of having older children is having the freedom to walk on the beach in the early morning hours without having to worry about the kids falling out of bed or leaping off the deck and spending the rest of your life with a large "G for Guilt" permanently etched into your forehead.

One morning my husband and I were walking on the beach, and let's just say this is one of the areas where we differ. I like to talk and walk, and he only likes to walk. This leaves me wondering if he is not listening or is perhaps even bored. When I walk with my female friends, they like to talk, and this is actually what makes the whole "get your heart rate up" thing bearable. But my husband does not like to talk, and I have to go to extremes to get him to do so while walking. It is a challenge indeed, but one that I enjoy.

So we're walking along the beach the next morning, and I notice he's picking up momentum which makes it harder for me to talk because I'm huffing and puffing, but I manage to rasp, "Hey, have you seen my right ear? It's actually getting crunchy!"

He picks up speed, and so do I. "Hey, look! I just peeled off an entire piece of my bottom lip!"

At that point he took off running, which in all fairness, he does most mornings, because he wants to be healthy. I want to be healthy, too, but my method is eating walnuts and an occasional pomegranate. I sat down in the sand and watched the ebb and flow and thought about what all of us would do for the rest of the day. With six laptops, numerous iPhones and iPods and Netflix movies, it was my mission to get the kids out of the house for at least an hour.

After a while my husband came jogging back down the beach, his heart rate up and his shirt soaked. "How you doing?" he asked.

"Fine," I replied. And then we began our walk back to the beach house, where he once again left me. "Hang on a minute!" I yelled. "I just broke off a piece of my crunchy ear."

"Well, you've always been Vincent van Gogh's biggest fan," he said. "Now you two have something in common. Hey, pass me some of that Bahama Mama lip repair. My lips are tender as a blankety-blank!"

I tossed him the Bahama Mama, and we enjoyed the rest of the day. Everyone went to the beach, no one stepped on a jellyfish or got tangled up in seaweed, and the sunscreen worked on all body parts.

Around day five of our vacation, we got a tad homesick this year. "Wonder what the cats are doing," I said.

"I don't know," said my husband. "They're probably outside chasing cicadas, or stretched out in our bed watching *Animal Planet* or *Nine Lives to Live*."

The next moment while we were walking on the beach, my husband slowed down and in a philosophical moment he asked, "What is your dream? What do you want to do for the rest of your life?"

"I want to eat fried okra and get paid for it," I said.

He picked up speed and shortly took off running, but that's okay because it's good for him to get his heart rate up, and I want him to be around for a long time.

Even if he does make fun of my crunchy ear.

## Birthday Tips

My birthday is coming up, and it is a biggie. In fact it is the biggest birthday I have ever had, but can't the same thing be said for all of us? Like I always say, Hey, I'm just happy to be here. But then again, I am a Leo. On the good side, we are loyal, gregarious, and generous. On the bad side, we are loud, proud, and egotistical, as some would have us believe. But what do they know?

Anyway, this particular birthday has me thinking, for it is a milestone. For women, everything gets complicated as we get older, and we have to get more and more creative if we yearn for the materialistic things in life.

Birthdays are a lot like Christmas. Depending on your age and your weight, you have to act real nice for a designated period of time before the big day comes. In my case, this has equaled an entire month, which will soon be over. During the course of the past decade, I have found the following tips to be tried and true, regardless of age:

- Nibble your man on the ear and whisper, "If Johnny Depp knocked on my door right now

with a box of chocolates and a dozen long-stemmed roses while wearing his wife-beater shirt, I would tell him to come back in ten years." Note: This one is very hard.
- Just for one day, do not talk to your husband about the six-hundred-pound woman in Florida whose body grafted into the couch. Ditto the woman who grew into her toilet seat. Do not say, "I can't believe this happened to a woman and not a man. Y'all are the ones who sit there on the commode looking at deer antlers and golf balls for five hours every morning."
- Change the sheets and buy a sexy new candle—get rid of that wickless, dusty, melted blob that has been sitting on your nightstand for five years.
- Brush, floss, use mouthwash, and clean your teeth with baking soda for a solid week. And don't forget to smile.
- For two entire weeks, stop sleeping in your clothes and slip into a sexy nightgown. Note: The faded Care Bear capris do not cut it.
- When life gets hard, make curtains out of your moo-moos.
- Exfoliate your entire body and sandblast your feet. In cases such as mine, a power washer is required.

- Dress up as Juliet, stand in a chair, and recite the balcony scene from *Romeo and Juliet* with heartfelt emotion and unquestionable talent. When your performance has ended, leap ever so lightly from the chair to the couch and purr in his ear like a small fluffy kitten. Lose fifty pounds before the big performance, and be sure to adorn the crown of your head with a handmade clover strand from your back yard.

That's all the advice I have to offer for now. It has worked so far, and hopefully, I will have more to offer in another milestone.

In the meantime, here's a toast to all the birthdays in the world, including Leos.

## Clarity Defined

I've never been fifty before, until today. It's true what they say about milestones: You look forward, you look back.

I woke up this morning and immediately thought, "I am fifty." I made a mental list of the ten worst things that have happened to me so far. Without question, they were easy to identify, easy to prioritize.

Then I made a mental list of the ten best things that have happened to me so far, but I got to ten and still had fifty more things to add to the list. This list was different.

I noticed that not a single item on my "top ten good things" list occurred before I married my husband and gave birth to our babies. And then I noticed that many of the items on the "top ten good things" list were seemingly small, but oh so significant.

Permanent images are embedded in my brain. That thunderstorm in front of our huge living room window out in Obion County, July 1984. In the stillness of the night, in the darkness of the corn, my husband and I watched the lightning light up the cornfields that surrounded our house out in West Tennessee. Soft rains and swaying corn, sweet smiles in the key of C with no minor chords struck.

The morning after our first child, Leah, was born was unprecedented and heavenly. The nurse brought her in and placed her on my stomach and I felt a love I had never felt. It was bliss, perfect bliss. All I could do was smile. I was smiling on the inside, smiling on the outside, and that smile was so powerful and so full of love that it carries me through the hard times to this day.

That was no accident.

Katy arrived in September 1985. When she was born, my husband looked at her and smiled and said, "Katy's got dimples." He still looks at her and smiles that same way. Another thunderstorm shut the power off that night, and baby Katy was in the hospital room with me. Lightning flickered, wind blew, rain fell, and the nurse came to get her, but I kept her with me instead. There is nothing in this world like your newborn baby sleeping beside you. I believe a piece of heaven falls from the sky and into the heart when a baby is born.

Patrick was born in September 1987. I had never had a baby boy before, never had a brother or many boy cousins, but I knew from the start that Patrick would be easy. He would answer many questions in my life. His little squinched-up face and full pouty lips still look the same sometimes. He cried when I sang to him and still he does not like music. He is a thinker who loves to watch the weather, especially thunderstorms.

Gus arrived in May 1991, the day of the Kentucky Derby. A big fat happy baby who smiled at the world when he was born. He liked to cuddle right from the start, and when Gus was born there was a party feel in the room. Lots of people, no complications. Just pure happiness once again.

So many memories, so many good times. I see Leah at her dance recitals, Katy riding her bicycle for the very first time. Patrick in first grade, standing with his back to us at Open House, while the other children faced their parents and sang. Gus with his blond hair and big smile, holding a soccer ball, pleased as punch. Gus at Dale Hollow Lake, hugging every single person before he leaves.

I like to believe that on some level, my experiences are universal to all parents. My contact with others tells me that they are.

It has been a good ride so far. The best of rides.

## Fifty Is the New Eighty

What is it about fifty? Something strange and unprecedented is happening in the world of the fifty-year-old, and I don't like it one little bit, because, well, I am a certain age and so is my husband and so are a lot of my friends whose names I will not mention unless they have offended me in some way in the past month.

Most recently, self-proclaimed King of Pop Michael Jackson grabbed the world's attention not because he was fifty, but because he was dead. According to a senior law enforcement official briefed on the initial investigation of Jackson's death, it's probable that drugs played a part. He told ABC News that Jackson was "heavily addicted" to the powerful pain killer Oxycontin and received "daily doses" of it and of another pain killer, Demerol.

Jackson was soon followed by fifty-year-old Billy Mays, the pitchman who turned me on to OxiClean. Mays liked to tell the story of giving bottles of OxiClean to the three hundred guests at his wedding and doing his ad spiel, "Powered by the air we breathe!" on the dance floor at the reception. Visitors to his house frequently got bottles of the grainy white particle cleaner along with various housekeeping tips.

Remember Bernie Mac? He recently died at age fifty due to complications from pneumonia.

The good news is, not all fifty-year-olds are dead. The bad news is our behavior is growing weirder by the minute. Take Keith Wright of New York, for instance, who disrobed during flight while sitting in his seat in the back of the aircraft. Wright was reportedly unresponsive when a flight attendant asked him repeatedly to get dressed, and he refused to be covered with a blanket. The cross-country US Airways flight was diverted to Albuquerque after Wright peeled out of his clothes and into his birthday suit.

When my twenty-one-year-old son heard about the recent status of the fifty-year-old, he said, "Well, I guess fifty's the new eighty." Was this supposed to be FUNNY?

In spite of the crisis, there is still hope: Madonna is fifty and is adopting her fiftieth child from Ethiopia, Darío Grandinetti is a fifty-year-old Argentine actor, Aaron Tippin is an American country music artist and record producer, Charlie Kaufman is an Academy Award winning screenwriter, producer, and director. And then there's my husband and my friends and me, of course, who with luck will make it to July 29 and cross the danger zone.

Truly, fifty has been a challenging year. I forgot my fourth child's name, I wore my shirt inside-out to the grocery store, and I developed a frozen shoulder which did lend itself to a little fun. On Facebook in response to the question, "What are you doing?" my frozen shoulder allowed me to reply, "I'm listening to 'Frozen Shoulder' by Lortab." And there are advantages to being in pain. For instance I constantly get to use my favorite line from *The Silence of the Lambs*: "It wants the lotion rubbed on its body."

This whole thing has changed my view of fifty. Rather than viewing it as old age, I'm just happy to be here, halfway sane and fully clothed.

## The Three Dead Dwarfs

The only compliment I have received since I got old is "Your optic nerve looks great!"

But that's okay, because I can now see things I haven't seen in ten years, thanks to my optometrist and my new contact lenses. Upon being able to simultaneously see up close and far away, I came home and read a book, minus the reading glasses. The next morning I went to work and e-mailed my hyperopic, myopic fast-walking friend. The one who scarfed up one hundred pairs of reading glasses at a yard sale.

"Have you seen that new kind of 'fattening' mascara that has the white stuff on one end and the black stuff (aka mascara) on the other end?" I wrote. "Well, I happen to have some of that fattening mascara. This morning I looked in the mirror after I got to work, and noticed that my eyelashes were white. I forgot to put the black stuff on!

"And that's not all. I got new contacts yesterday—that new kind that works on both nearsightedness and farsightedness. In other words, I can now see. The problem is, after I looked in the mirror, I realized I not only needed mascara, but also a face lift, an eyebrow transplant, a root job, a haircut, and a whole new beauty regimen.

"I wanted you to be the first to know about the Mascara Tip of the Day. White eyelashes rock!"

She saw me shortly thereafter and cackled, "It looks like your eyelashes have been singed. I have some mascara—I'll send it your way." I waited, but the mascara never arrived because she forgot where she put it, citing some excuse like, "Just when the answer pops into my head, I forget what the question was."

Lately it seems my friends and I are in the same boat, and it is sinking. Question is, will we remember how to swim?

But it's OK, because I can see. No longer will my optometrist be able to snicker and say, "Follow the white coat." But I'd better not say too much about him here, because he is the one who so kindly restored my vision. Not to mention the lecture I might get about the sharing of mascara.

Looking back, a lot of things are beginning to make sense. Like the day I told my hubby, "Well, it sure looked like Colgate to me," after he'd brushed his teeth with the cortisone cream I handed to him. "At least your gums won't itch," I said.

He looked at me as if I had an idiot trapped inside myself, clawing to get out. I said to him, "Even Helen Keller would have seen that look you just gave me."

"Could you go for one day without mentioning Helen Keller, William Faulkner, and Edgar Allan Poe? Just one day?" he asked.

"OK, I admit it," I said. "I am obsessed with Helen Keller, William Faulkner, and Edgar Allan Poe. The three dead dwarfs: Blind, Drunk, and Crazy. I promise not to talk about them anymore. I'll just write about them instead."

Now that I can see, the possibilities are endless. Like reading *The Raven* without the glasses. Edgar would be proud.

## Masterpieces

From my basement, I hear Pink Floyd drifting up from the computer, and I smile because I know we've gone full circle. My kids can play "Comfortably Numb" full blast, because I like masterpieces. The fact that today's kids are listening to "Comfortably Numb," "Stairway to Heaven," and "Tangled Up in Blue" tells me they recognize masterpieces themselves.

But masterpieces also encompass everyday experiences, such as snooping through your mother's Sunday purse for a piece of Juicy Fruit when you are a child and hanging upside down from the dogwood tree in your front yard in July. Seeing the vastness of the ocean and smelling the salty breeze for the first time is a masterpiece, and so is a family.

A family is a work in progress, and the main artists are the parents, who, if they are smart, learn when to erase and change the colors and the brushes in search of balance and contrast. If necessary, they will rip up the portrait and burn it and start all over if need be, because smart parents know when something is terribly wrong with the picture. Generally speaking, if the picture looks perfect in the early days of family, it makes a great fire starter.

Things change. There was a time when reality terrified me, but now it is my greatest comfort. I am way past the early days of marriage when leaving and cleaving and becoming one were the ideal. Now, I believe it's OK for our parents to want to spend time with their children minus their spouses, because it takes them back to their own sweet days of their early parenthood, and gives them a chance to reminisce. And while I believe the idea of becoming one has merit, I have found it impossible and unhealthy to completely meld with my husband, because we are different, and that is okay.

After twenty-two years of marriage, he tells me he wants to sail around the world, and if he's going to sail around the world, I can at least become a famous rock star. And though these possibilities are remote, dreams are the ultimate masterpiece.

When I compare our conversations of then and now, I see art. Consider this marital scene:

"What makes you think you look like a codger?" I ask.

"I looked in the mirror," he says.

"Well, I'm getting old, too."

"Yeah, but you don't look like a codger."

"That's because I wear makeup and dye my hair. Also my name means 'forever fun.' Yours means 'battleship warrior and sounder of trumpets,'" I say.

"But in the book of life, you ain't turned a page in fifty years," he says.

"That's because I'm only forty-five," I say.

The words my children say are pretty pictures, hanging in my mind. My youngest, whose diet consists of five foods, loves Kentucky Fried Chicken. A couple of years ago when I bought him a breast meal at the drive-through, he smiled and said, "Heaven is inside that box." The kid knows a masterpiece when he sees it.

Granny's journal was a masterpiece because she jotted down lines that were so sparse they somehow revealed much more. Oh, she never told much, and that is why her words were so powerful: "September 3, 1963: Sister and Irene drove up and picked some turnip greens this afternoon." "July 20, 1976: I'm worried about Jane."

My writing is wordier than Granny's, and if I switched to her minimalistic style my journal would look like this: "November 3, 2008: The mopping did not go well." "March 17, 2013: Not a good day for a thong."

Due to today's high-tech weather equipment, we are rarely surprised by snow. But today, on St. Patrick's Day, I woke up amazed to see the ground painted in white, a true masterpiece.

Don't wait to paint your masterpieces. Open your eyes wide and look around; look behind you, look ahead, and you will see them in full view.

## Rock Band

The other day I was standing among a group of seventh-graders, when one of them asked me, "Were you born before the Internet?"

"Yes, I was born before Atari, the Nintendo duck shooter, and Pong," I said.

Gasps and horror filled the air. Whispers bounced across the room and into my ears. Phrases like, "Gotta be at least eighty," and "No wonder she forgets what day it is."

"Pong?" one of them asked. "Are you serious?"

"Of course, I'm serious," I said. "Pong was the greatest video game of its time. But now I'm into Rock Band. Every night I set it up in my den and belt out "Tangled Up in Blue" at the top of my lungs while my husband plays lead guitar."

This got their attention, and they sat and stared at me in semi-concern, mouths gaped. One of them whispered to the kid beside him, "She knows what Rock Band is," as if I had a conspiracy stuffed up my sleeve.

And I was thinking to myself, "They know who Bob Dylan is." That's a good thing, even if they were too young to appreciate the man. It warmed my heart to know they had heard not only of Bob Dylan, but also Atari, The Nintendo Duck, and Pong.

I heard one of them whisper, "She may just be seventy."

And then he asked me, "Do you really play Rock Band? Why do you play Rock Band? Aren't you supposed to be knitting or crocheting or something like that? Rock Band is what WE play."

"It's a free country," I said, "at least for the next few months. And for your information, I played Guitar Hero before I moved on to Rock Band."

Complete astonishment clouded the room. "You know about Guitar Hero?" he asked.

"I know a lot more than you think I know," I said, "and so does every other grown-up you've ever laid eyes on. Don't underestimate us."

"Why did you move on to Rock Band?" he asked, this time with true intrigue.

"Rock Band has basically replaced air guitar," I said. "With Rock Band you can invite your friends over and jam after a hard days' work. Now all my rowdy friends get down and play. Afterward, we drink hazelnut lattes and devour Junior Mints."

Together, we all laughed and shared in an integration of the generations, bonded by the very glue of technology that some people fear. I am not one of those people. What I am afraid of is the REAL music that's out there these days.

Take the recent Country Music Awards, for example, which very much resembled Rock Band with its animated singers, the contrived moves, the horrendous outfits, and most of all the belief of the singers that they not only could sing, but were actually belting out quality material.

What would Dylan say?

I believe that if the Nintendo Duck could shoot back, he would obliterate the set of the Country Music Awards and blow the "artists" all the way back to their roots that originally consisted of genuine threads of hardship, heartbreak, pain, and the cold hard truth.

Long ago in a faraway land, those folk roots were as authentic as honey in a comb, or snow by a creek in the woods in December. Today, those roots are every bit as shallow as the singers in Rock Band, who uncannily resemble today's real deal.

I'll take a plastic Dylan over a real Brad Paisley any day of the year.

## Mr. Clean

I cannot remember a time without Mr. Clean, and I keep a bottle of the big man underneath my kitchen sink, just for nostalgic purposes. Recently, I saw a TV commercial, and I noticed that Mr. Clean had burly white eyebrows. How could this be? After all these years, why was I just now noticing the burly whites? Was it possible that like the rest of the aging male population, Mr. Clean could be turning into a codger?

Never! Icons like Mr. Clean never change, and that is why I love them so. With luck, he will still be living in my house with his arms crossed and his eyebrows burly when I am old and gray. My children and grandchildren and possibly even my great-grandchildren will also be loyal to Mr. Clean, and perhaps one day we will sit around the fire and reminisce about the good old days and how he was always there for us.

My college son was recently home for Spring Break, and I'd made him some pancakes for breakfast. I decided to get fancy and clean off the kitchen counter, but Mr. Clean was nowhere to be found.

"Where's Mr. Clean?" I screamed.

"He fled," said my son. "He got tired of being used."

This is the son who spent eighteen years of his life talking to me for a total of three minutes on the telephone. After he became college bound, he transformed, and now he calls me every day. Recently, he called in the most serious of tones and asked, "How often should I clean my bathroom, Mom?"

I was at a loss for words and realized I was void of any set pattern of cleaning my bathrooms throughout the years.

"I don't know," I said. "Once a week, I guess."

Truth is, I've only let Mr. Clean out of the closet three or four times in my life. I like knowing he's there, but in a real crunch I have found baking soda to be my sweetest shine.

A few days passed and still I wondered: Had Mr. Clean's eyebrows always been burly and white? The answer is yes. I did a little research and discovered it was no wonder I could not remember a time without Mr. Clean, because he and I were both produced in the same year! His parents were Procter & Gamble, and in Europe, he is known as "Mr. Proper."

In Spain Mr. Clean is known as Don Limpio, and in Mexico he is called Maestro Limpio. After I discovered that Mr. Clean was regal and world-famous, I rescued him from the dank air underneath my kitchen sink and placed him on a shelf beside the Clabber Girl Baking Powder, the Watkins Vanilla Flavoring, and the Morton Salt.

After my in-depth study of Mr. Clean, I am convinced that I have been swayed for many reasons. The combination of his tight muscle shirt, his confidently crossed arms, and the expression on his face that says, "Prop your feet up, babe. I'll take care of EVERYTHING." In fact, Mr. Clean's logo is "Mr. Clean cleans your whole house and everything that's in it."

I'm waiting, big man.

# HOLIDAY CONFESSIONS

### Rabbit, Rabbit

I called my sister this morning.

"Happy New Year!" she said. "Don't you just adore the Tournament of Roses? I just love to look at the floats and the flowers and the vibrant colors. The pinks and the reds and all the little petals on the rosebuds—every year they just get more and more exquisite. Don't you just love it? You are watching it, aren't you?"

Apparently the bubbly was still in the champagne. Or maybe she's becoming more and more like our mother.

"No, I've never watched the Tournament of Roses in my entire life. I lost all interest in parades when Santa Claus stopped throwing out candy. I think the Tournament of Roses is boring and pretentious."

"You're kidding!" she said. "Well, I just love it."

"I understand. What are you going to do today?"

"Oh, I'll probably go work out. I always exercise on New Year's Day. It makes me feel so good. What are you going to do?"

"Wash clothes."

"Oh, no! You can't wash clothes on New Year's! You'll wash somebody out!"

"I'll what?"

"You'll wash somebody out. Back in 1995, Kay's grandmother told her never to wash clothes on New Year's because she would wash somebody out. Kay didn't heed the warning, and two weeks later, Aunt Ora dropped dead in the utility room, holding a load of wet rags. A week after that, her cousin Sue was pecked by a flock of wild geese and died all alone in the woods."

"Does this work on cats?" I asked.

"This is not a laughing matter," said Sis. "You do recall what happened to our mother, don't you?"

"Do you mean to tell me you washed Mama out back in 1987? Was it Tide or Cheer?"

"No, I didn't wash Mama out. It was the cedar tree."

"What are you talking about?"

"Mama always warned me never to plant a cedar tree in the yard, or somebody would die within the year. I didn't believe her, and in the spring of the year, she was gone."

"Yes, I recall that," I said. "So you're telling me you killed Mama with a cedar tree. Do you realize you could get sued for this and get all kinds of publicity? You could be on Oprah, Dateline, and maybe even Martha Stewart."

"This is not a good thing. Besides, Martha's not a talk show host. She's an insider trader with a flair for getting ten thousand people to disguise her as a decorator. Anybody who can pull off making a gingerbread house with Miss Piggy is a genius."

"Yeah, you're right. But she's great with greenery, like pines and cedars. This has Martha written all over it. She could even start her own cedar casket line."

"Make light of it if you wish," said Sis. "But I do hope you said 'rabbit, rabbit' when you woke up first thing this morning. You know that'll bring you good luck for the whole month of January."

"Not only did I utter the words 'rabbit, rabbit,' I am going to have good luck for the entire year, because I uttered the words 'white rabbit, white rabbit.' It's in the bag."

"You're kidding," said Sis. "I always forget to say 'rabbit, rabbit' on the first day of the month, even though you've been telling me to do this for years. I'll bet this is why I've had three root canals, asthma, and termites."

"I'm sure it is. But here's the trick: You have to say 'rabbit, rabbit' on the first day of the month, as soon as you wake up. No other words can be spoken before 'rabbit, rabbit,' or it won't work. I've said 'rabbit, rabbit' first thing on the first day of every month since 1992, except for February of '96. A tragedy indeed."

"What happened?" asked Sis.

"Horrors. Hemorrhoids, hail damage, Mormon invasion, and a root canal. Never again will I forget those two little words."

"Well, there's always February," said Sis. "Maybe I can make it through January without locusts or Bubonic Plague."

"I hope so. And please, no more cedar trees."

"Don't worry. It's awful, living with the guilt."

January second sounds like a great day for washing clothes.

## Valentine's Day

I stay about a holiday behind, but I'm doing better this year. Today is Valentine's Day, and I have already put away my snowman décor. And so it seems only fitting that I should write a column about Valentine's Day that will be published the day after the big love fest.

Many of us have reached that point in life where we are at a loss for ideas on Valentine's Day. Somehow the phrase "Big Momma's hot" does not mean what it used to. Oh, I tried, all right. Last week I browsed through Cool Springs in search of a romantic card and some cute pink pajamas, but there were men lurking in Victoria's Secret. All I can say is the only thing worse than seeing a man in Victoria's Secret is seeing a man in a turtleneck in Victoria's Secret.

The only man who should be allowed in Victoria's Secret is Johnny Depp, period. And so it was that I fled the store and the mall and the entire town after seeing the man in the turtleneck in Victoria's Secret, and I decided to seek alternate routes for Valentine's Day this year. After twenty-five years of marriage, the roses fade, the chocolate melts, and the lingerie doesn't look the same because they just don't make it like they used to.

Luckily, the muse came to my rescue and instructed me to write my own special greeting card for my husband. I have narrowed it down to two choices: "Baby you're so hot you feel like you just popped out of the toaster," or "They say it's better to give than to receive. So what're you going to give me?" I have the whole day ahead of me, and I know my heart will guide me in the right direction by the time he gets home from work.

Yes, things have changed in twenty-five years. The first year we were married, my husband sent me two dozen red roses and had them delivered to me at work. My long-time-married co-workers swooned and swarmed like bees and smiled a knowing smile and gouged each other in the side. "What was that all about?" I asked.

"Get a good long whiff of those roses and take a picture of them when you get home," said Trudy, "because the honeymoon will end before you know it, and he won't be sending you roses on Valentine's Day."

Hogwash! They obviously did not know MY husband, the man to whom I had been blissfully wed for two entire months. Nevertheless, when I got home that day, I had him take a picture of me holding the two dozen red roses, while posing in front of our brand new couch in our brand new house, a year before the brand new baby arrived.

Every year on Valentine's Day I look at that picture and smile my own knowing smile. Trudy was right, but that's okay because I never liked roses anyway. I preferred babies, so we had four of them. Tonight, two of them are going out with us to celebrate Valentine's Day, and to avoid the crowds we are going to eat at Steak and Shake.

Yes, a vanilla milkshake has replaced the red roses, and there's a song in there somewhere. I'm just a practical, yet unconventional, girl, who likes to celebrate Valentine's Day and other holidays in various and sundry ways.

So far it's working.

## Ghostbusters

Back in my childhood days, Halloween was a night on which kids would throw a sheet over their heads, cut eyes in it, and run out the door with a brown paper bag from H.G. Hill that would be filled to the brim with candy by the end of the evening.

There was no talk of tainted apples or poison candy, and there was certainly no talk of Halloween being a day to worship the Devil.

Back then, things were simpler, and grown-ups had more to do than to sit around and twiddle their thumbs, wondering what holiday they could mess up next. Today it seems we have too many grown-ups who have time to sit around and ponder the origin of things, such as holidays.

I am not one of those grown-ups. Halloween is my favorite holiday, and it always has been and always will be. For years I have dressed up as a clown on Halloween and passed out candy to the trick-or-treaters, but I'm tired of the clown thing. The polka-dots are faded, and the hat is torn, and I hate that stupid nose. I've changed. This year,

I've ordered a French Maid costume from Frederick's of Hollywood, complete with six-inch spike heels and fishnet stockings, and I plan to surprise my husband, dressed in this garb with a bucket of Almond Joys and Sugar Babies, his favorite. I'll do the tricks, and he'll get the treats, and I might just get a new red convertible Volkswagen Bug out of the whole deal.

Of course, I'll probably wear the clown suit while passing out the candy to the trick-or-treaters, or I might be a vampire. That way, I could leave on the black-eye makeup when I slip into my French Maid costume later in the evening. Just take out the fangs, and I'll be set to go.

And another thing, the local animal shelter has put a ban on the adoption of black and white cats, which is fine by me. But why doesn't the kitty cult go after the deviant Siamese? Every year for the past six years, I have put a sign around my Siamese cat's neck that says "Maim me, I'm yours," yet no one has taken her. It's not fair. This year, I'm going to crown her with a set of devil horns and see if I have any luck.

Also, the Ghost Walk that is planned for Saturday night at Rose Hill Cemetery has been mainly praised, but also criticized as disrespect to the deceased who are buried there. Lord willing, I will be at that Ghost Walk, taking the tour and listening to the stories and paying my respects to those gone before me. I like to think that when I'm dead and gone, people will think enough of me to saunter across the grounds of my resting place and remember me with tales and stories. Ghosts deserve a little attention, too.

Today we live in a world in which people have a need to be critical, an era in which people have enough time on their hands to sit around and conjure up whiny thoughts and deeds. It's too bad these people can't get a life and enjoy it like the rest of us.

You never know if this Halloween may be your last. And for that reason, I plan to max out in my French Maid costume and live it up while I've got the chance. Could mean a drive down Highway One, overlooking the Pacific in my new red convertible Volkswagen Bug. We'll see.

## Halloween Fun

Halloween was different this year.

Maybe it was the full moon.

Maybe it was all that chocolate.

Maybe I'm crazy.

I simply don't know what it was that possessed me to slip on my Freddy Krueger mask and stalk naked in front of my husband. I got a rush out of clawing at his neck and making guttural noises from deep in my throat, but I may have gone too far this time.

He covered his eyes and screamed, "Get that thing off! I'll never get this picture out of my head! Why do you do these things?"

What's wrong with him? I mean, it's not like I spent all the money, or ate all the pecans. I was just having a little Halloween fun.

Last night my husband slept with the nightlight on and a flashlight tucked beneath his pillow. But I've already figured out what I can do to make up for this trauma that I have inflicted upon him. I'll go out and buy a Marilyn Monroe mask and stalk him again. That should work. I might even sing "Happy Birthday" to him and jump out of a cake.

Aside from my impulsive moment of passionate gore, Halloween was still different this year.

Trick-or-treaters were sparse, and something in the air just didn't seem right. It reminded me somewhat of the Halloween of 1982, when trick-or-treating was canceled because of the tainted Tylenol scare.

Halloween has always been one of my favorite holidays, especially since I've had children.

I love all the little witches and devils that walk up the steps to my front door and say, "Trick or treat." I love my pumpkin jar that I fill with candy corn each year, and I love my King Kong mask that I wear with my clown suit.

One of my favorite Halloween traditions is to recite a children's poem that goes something like this:

"Five little pumpkins, sitting on a gate; the first one says, 'Oh, my—it's getting late!' The second one says, 'There are witches in the air!' The third one says, 'We don't care!' The fourth one says, 'Let's run and run and run!' The fifth one says, 'It's time for Halloween fun!'

Whewwwwww went the wind, and OUT went the lights, and the five little pumpkins rolled out of sight."

Every year I set my five little pumpkins on my windowsill and recite "Five Little Pumpkins" as often as my family can stomach it.

My Halloween wish for this year is that many parents and children will learn and remember this enchanting Halloween poem and pass it on for generations to come. May "Five Little Pumpkins" become a Halloween tradition that outlives Freddy Krueger and Sir Cecil Creep.

Halloween is a fun time to unleash your creativity, as I so uniquely did this year. The holiday should be associated with children, trick-or-treating, candy, Jack-O-Lanterns, mischievous fun and bobbing for apples—not evil and darkness and religious misconceptions. Those groups who oppose Halloween have every right to do so, but they'll never stop me from slipping into my Halloween maniac mode.

Thanksgiving is our next big holiday.

Wonder where I could find a turkey mask?

### Tasty Bake Oven

Thanksgiving's over and Christmas is coming and I still see a Jack-o-lantern on my dining room table. Whenever I look at Jack, he has this sneering smile that seems to say, "Do I look like Santa Claus?" And then he laughs his maniacal Jack-o-lantern laugh, and I vow to decorate for Christmas that very night.

The Girl Scout motto flashes through my brain: "Be prepared." And then I remember the trauma of my Girl Scout experience, and I ditch the guilt faster than Santa goes up the chimney. Things have been busy lately. Still, we have to have Christmas. It only comes once a year—the mistletoe, the peppermint, the tree in the middle of the floor.

Sometimes, just looking at Christmas pictures inspires me to decorate, so I sit down on the couch with the Christmas photo albums and reminisce about days gone by. And then I take a closer look. Did our tree really look like that back in 1989? Had it been damaged by a glacier? Did we find it on the side of the road? And why was the popcorn strung only halfway down the tree?

I see another picture and put on my reading glasses and hold it up under the light. Was my son really wearing his Batman pajamas on Christmas Eve? I hear a cackle coming from my dining room table, and Jack is laughing out loud. I begin to plan his demise, when suddenly, I am flooded with memories, and I realize that no matter what is on my dining room table, nothing can take them away.

It was the Christmas of 1987, a hard year in many ways. My mother had died unexpectedly, and we had two small children and a brand new baby. It was the pre-Internet and Cool Springs era, and that year we did most of our shopping from the Sears catalog. When the boxes arrived at our house, we would discreetly transfer them to a closet in my husband's office.

My older daughter had talked incessantly about her longing for the Tasty Bake Oven, and it was the first thing we ordered, along with an array of Tasty Bake cake mixes and cookware. It was the year of the Puffalump and Teddy Ruxpin, but the biggie was the Tasty Bake Oven.

It is also significant that this was the only child who could actually talk and possibly remember what she did or did not get, and these were the days when I was still sucked in by the guilt of the Girl Scout motto.

Christmas Eve arrived, and we tucked the kids into bed with visions of sugarplums in their heads, and we opened the boxes we had hidden in my husband's office. There were tons of boxes, some large, and we assumed that our order was intact. Horrors! Of all things, the Tasty Bake Oven was missing! However, the array of Tasty Bake mixes and cookware were there, all shiny and new.

My emotions became a kaleidoscope of Girl Scout failure, motherhood failure, and complete failure as a human being. I looked in the mirror and saw Charles Manson with a smile on his face.

My husband was reassuring and calm, and I realized there was nothing we could do until it hit me: Santa could write a note, explaining that the Tasty Bake was too large and too special to be flown by his reindeer, and that he had made special arrangements for it to be delivered at Toys r Us the day after Christmas.

Christmas morning arrived, and our oldest came flying out to see her new Tasty Bake Oven. I peeped out behind my hands and watched as she sized up the situation and said, "Well, I still got my Tasty Bake mixes."

"Look!" I said. "It's a NOTE!" I read her the note from Santa and she swallowed it hook, line, and sinker. Since the other kids could not even talk, they were not emotionally scarred in the least. The morning was spent with Teddy Ruxpin, Puffalumps, stockings filled to the brim, and a great breakfast of homemade biscuits, sausage, and sawmill gravy.

Now some people might ask why we didn't look in the boxes before putting them under the tree. Some people might scoff at our glacier-stricken tree, and some people would cringe at the Batman pajamas on Christmas Eve.

But guess what? I don't care anymore. I am proud to be a Girl Scout reject, and I now have my own motto: "Be flexible."

Works for me.

## Jeggings

It's the Christmas season, that most wonderful time of the year, and in an attempt to avoid hauling the holiday decor down from the attic, I go shopping every afternoon.

Day before yesterday I was in a dressing room at T.J. Maxx when the cell phone next door to me rang to the tune of "Jingle Bell Rock," and the conversation went like this: "Hello? You can eat some spaghetti. You can heat it up. Well, you can start. Shut up, Zachary. I'll be there when I get there. Don't start it." Click.

Isn't the joy of Christmas wonderful?

I stared at my heap of clothing and prayed for my personal shopper angel to appear and sprinkle some fairy dust over everything I had chosen. Sure, those skinny jeans looked skinny—that's why they were called skinny jeans. It was all an illusion, I assured myself. Why, Aunt Jemima herself could squeeze into those things and have plenty of room for another stack of pancakes. Upon further inspection I realized they were not skinny jeans, they were jeggings, and I recalled a Facebook chat I had with my daughter a while back.

Aside from rotting out the interior lining of your cranium, Facebook chats offer certain benefits, such as column potential and escape from reality. When I told my daughter I'd bought a pair of jeggings, she said, "Jeggings! I forgot that was a thing. Nineties fashion is coming back, you know. Remember belly shirts?"

"What are belly shirts?" I asked.

"Don't get one," she said. "They're short-cropped shirts that show your tummy."

"I think flat bellies always look stylish, don't you?" I said.

"Sure, if you have one, and if you're wearing a bathing suit," she said. "You're just not supposed to show your belly in public. It looks trashy."

I said, "You sound like my mother using the word 'trashy.' First I spend the formative years of my life with my mother telling me what to wear, and now you've taken her place. Goodnight, Mother Teresa. I'll text you tomorrow."

I snapped back to reality and looked down at the little jeggings that were staring up at me with pleading eyes, as if they wanted to run out in search of Twiggy. The girl next door was gone, probably chopping up her husband and putting him in the freezer for eating all the spaghetti. Who would know if the jeggings did not work out for me?

Just like the hokey-pokey, I put my right leg in, and I tried to take it out but it was stuck. Someone had put Super Glue in my jeggings. I twisted and turned, writhing in pain and despair, picturing the fire department breaking down the door with the fireman saying, "Lady, your little toe is bigger than that entire leg. What were you thinking?"

Finally, I escaped from the jeggings and whispered something horrible into the fake pocket on the back. I put them on the little hanger and quietly exited the dressing room.

"Did these work out for you?" asked the sales clerk.

"Nah," I said. "A little loose."

So I ventured over to the shoe store, thinking a new pair of boots would be a great way to end my day. Somehow I knocked over every pair in the store and could not get those cardboard inserts back in to save my life. Finally I found the perfect pair but the zipper was stuck, and they had to get three men and a baby to detach the shoplifting detector from those suckers.

I didn't really want them anyway, and I'd forgotten all about the whole thing, when I heard them cheer, "Yay! We got them! We got the zipper going! Do you want to try them on?"

What could I say, other than yes?

I ended up buying the boots out of the goodness of my heart, and the next morning when I stuck my right foot in, it would not come back out, just like the hokey-pokey. The zipper was stuck, and I was late for work, and there was a ceramic pumpkin staring at me from the dining room table, when it was supposed to be a gingerbread house or a giant porcelain elf.

Finally, I escaped from the boots and made it to work on time and promptly returned them to the shoe store that afternoon.

Today, I am going to put on my husband's sweat pants, take the ceramic pumpkin back to the attic, and haul out the porcelain elf and set it on the dining room table. It's a start.

## Jest 'Fore Christmas

*"But thinking of the things yer'd like to see upon that tree*
*Jest 'fore Christmas be as good as yer kin be!"*

—Eugene Field, Poet (1850-1895)

One of my favorite parts of childhood was the set of Childcraft Books that sat firm and square in the blond bookcase in the den. Although there was a complete set, there were only three books that interested me: the arts and crafts book, the poetry book, and the music book.

I wore the arts and crafts book out about the same time I wore my mother out, begging her to help me make all those artsy projects with glitter and glue and glee. I could just envision us together in the kitchen with our aprons on, me standing in a chair while we stirred homemade Play-Doh over the sink, while singing "Joy to the World."

But my dream was my mother's nightmare. Whenever I would clomp into the kitchen holding the Childcraft arts and crafts book, she would turn green and look out the window, while I begged her relentlessly to whip out the aprons and the cornstarch and the food coloring and the SALT. It was the salt that excited me most. The thought of dumping an entire can of the Morton Girl into a pan with other ingredients and turning her into glue just thrilled me to no end. In my mind, it was something akin to cooking Lot's wife, who as we all know had looked back and turned into a pillar of salt.

I almost got my mother to say yes one time, but she got the best of me by saying, "Hon, why don't you go read the Childcraft poetry book? Be sure and read the poem 'Jest 'Fore Christmas.' It reminds me of you."

So off I flew in search of the Childcraft poetry book, where I quickly flipped over to the poem "Jest 'Fore Christmas" by Eugene Field. The pictures were adorable, and I was immediately hooked on the poem. That is until I actually read the words, which clearly came straight from the book of Revelation.

"Horrors!" I thought to myself, as I slammed the book shut, then peeked at it again just in case it might be true. It is no coincidence that this is the identical method I used after looking at the pictures in the book *A Child is Born*, when I was pregnant with my first child. The picture in that sadistic book that made me "slam and peek" was the one of the baby being born, yet it was only halfway in this world when it was first captured on film. Imagine having to smile and say "cheese" when you're only halfway out.

Basically, the theme of "Jest 'Fore Christmas" is that one must be good in order to get any Christmas presents. As usual, I was faced with the ultimate "or else" dilemma: What if one had NOT been good? Even at an early age, I suspected my behavior was not good, because I was having so much fun all the time. Plus, there were occasional mentions of switches and chunks of coal in the stocking. Add to that the story of Lot's wife, which I heard frequently in church. It was easy to put these worries on the back burner until Christmas rolled around.

I realized it was impossible for me to stuff eleven months of bad into one month of good, so I did what any healthy person would do: I gave up and prayed hard.

Perhaps the biggest miracle of Christmas is that it worked for me then and it works for me now. I never did get switches or chunks of coal in my stocking, and my mother never made Play-doh with me out of the Morton Girl.

But she did teach me that even when you're bad, a powerful force still loves you, and she also introduced me to a lot of good poetry.

## Fire

One of the best parts about winter is the fireplace. Not only does it provide the warm and cozy idyllic family scene, it is a nifty place to burn up those items you no longer want or need. Yes, when it comes to winter, my motto is, "Burn that thing up! Watch the orange peelings melt into blue! Engulf that Christmas picture from the district manager in Chicago—the one you never met—watch his wig go up in flames!"

My children were recently home for Christmas, all gathered together in the den while I was trying to get the fire started one cold frosty morn. There were no twigs, there were no pine cones, and there were certainly no fire starters, so I did what any logical person would do. I tossed a lightweight cotton shirt into the fire, in place of kindling.

"But Mom, that's my favorite shirt!" my daughter exclaimed.

"Aw, you can always get another one," I said. "Heck, I'll even pay for it. Just look at this fire!"

Later that day I envisioned myself in an infomercial, holding a pillow and standing in front of a fire, saying, "Is your pillow grimy and flat? Burn it up and sniff the toxic fumes before it is too late! And nothing you have ever heard about Styrofoam is remotely true!"

That night on my Facebook status I wrote, "I have a far in the farplace" and got fifteen responses, all POSITIVE. And that is merely one of the things I love about the South.

The next morning my husband was poking around in the ashes. "What's this egg shell doing in here?" he asked.

"I threw them in there," I said. "They're organic. Actually, when you think about it, EVERYTHING is organic."

"Do you think your hormone therapy is still working?" he asked.

"Of course, it is," I said. Now toss me that paper mache Christmas gnome off the mantel. I've wanted to do this for years."

"Here," he said, lifting the poker from my hand. "Let me sit there a minute."

If there's one thing I've learned in our twenty-eight years of marriage, it's that fire fights are right up there with food fights and "Here, I'll drive" fights. In truth, fire fights are even worse because the cave man mentality kicks in and all things feminine are not only diminished but instantly nuked. Everyone knows men know how to build the perfect fire from a couple of wet twigs in the middle of an igloo at the bottom of an avalanche.

So I gave him the poker and let him have his fun, while envisioning the Christmas trash I would burn as soon as he left for the office. Those Styrofoam packing peanuts are hard to find, but somehow I ended up with a box full of the pastel green ones, and if I burned them, it would be impossible for them to inhabit the landfills for light years to come.

It's a hard job, but somebody has to do it.

## Lilacs and Petunias

I just couldn't help it. There he was sitting all alone, so I went over and sat down beside him on the floor and crossed my legs, Indian-style. The mall was deserted and the Christmas gnomes were standing still and the dancing bear was plugged in tight to the battery recharger, and suddenly, I was alone with Santa, in a fluff of red and green.

"Ho! Ho! Ho!" he said. "And what do YOU want for Christmas?"

"You can't give me the things I want," I said, "but still I yearn for them."

"Try me," said Santa. "You might be surprised."

"I want my mama, I want a new song from Johnny Mercer and Billie Holiday, and I'd like to write an old-timey song . . . something like 'And Now I Think of You.' I'm in a real time warp here, Santa."

"Go on," he said, lighting his pipe and kicking off his black boots. His bare feet were firm and tan, and his toenails were nicely groomed. Young feet.

"I thought you were supposed to be old and fat and jolly," I said, "but here you've got nice tanned toes and a good pedicure."

"This ain't about me," he said. "It's about you. What else is on your mind?"

I sat and stared straight ahead at the eight reindeer and the three-foot candy canes stuck in the floor, wondering what was holding them up, and suddenly, I had the urge to open up to Santa and tell him things I couldn't even say to myself.

"I feel like last year's boots and yesterday's paper," I said, "and at night I dream of earthworms and bulls. Also, there's this stupid line that keeps running through my head— *Lord I cried when Dumbo died.* And lately I've been thinking they should start making Pepto-Bismol in different colors, like neon green or horse-hair brown."

"Go on," said Santa, with his head thrown back, staring at the roof of his portable gazebo.

"Things drive me crazy," I said. "Things like ice-chomping, lip-smacking, apple-crunching and mispronunciation of words. I work with a man who says 'dramastic' all the time, and he thinks it's really a word. And it terrifies me that not one of our presidents has ever been able to pronounce 'nuclear.' Also, I despise acrylic sweaters, plastic geese, and Tide commercials."

"Anything else?" said Santa.

"Yeah, there's another woman I work with—a religious zealot, always passing out 'Journey with Jesus' brochures and angels and crosses and such. The thing is, she's been married five times and thinks she's holding the one ticket to heaven. She's always been on a crusade for Christ, but when it comes to getting lonely, Jesus sits on the back burner with the stove turned off."

"I see," said Santa, exhaling with a smile. "Is there anything you like?"

"Yeah," I said. "I like old friends and old pianos, warm oatmeal cookies, tulips, and Hank Williams songs. I like eating pancakes in the middle of the night, skinny-dipping, soft summer rain, blackberry cobbler, fried okra, white teeth, pink lips, massages, Jacuzzis, big juicy steaks, and old red bicycles. And then there's 'The Wizard of Oz,' Beethoven, lilacs, and petunias. I like a good cry, playing in the sand with my kids, and walking along the beach with my husband at night in July."

Santa wiggled his attractive toes and sat up. "Go home now," he said. "Curl up on the couch and watch *Dumbo* and have yourself a good cry. Kiss your children goodnight and snuggle up with your husband before you drift off to sleep, for tonight you may dream of lilacs and petunias."

"No more earthworms and bulls?" I asked.

"Time will tell," said Santa. "After all, it's only a dream. You've got some pretty good realities here—cling to them while you can."

Lilacs and petunias?

I can sleep on that.

## Bubbles

Here in the midst of the holiday season, I was making a vat of sausage balls, which sent me on a quest for a sharp knife. I settled for a dull knife and started sawing away and uttering phrases other than "Merry Christmas" and "You are the sunshine of my life."

My husband yelled from the den, "Be careful cutting that sausage . . . all we need is a severed limb."

This is my prayer for the new year: If men can't have babies, let them have hot flashes. Amen.

A severed limb? Oh, I am not even going to get started on that comment. I'll just focus on the prayer.

Everybody complains about the commercialization of Christmas, and I agree so wholeheartedly that in my front yard, I have an inflatable Winnie the Pooh on a Harley, holding a sign that says, "Santa ain't real and neither am I."

Commercialism aside, the season does have its upside. Children, for instance. It is fun watching the little children open their presents while the parents wonder when the money is going to rain down from the sky. Actually the parents don't wonder about this until January, because there is a certain numbness that accompanies Christmas spending. It is God's way of helping us survive.

One of my favorite Christmas memories is the year my son received a battery-powered Jeep that was worth more than the car I drove at the time. It was red, shiny, and new, and it was a beauty. Of all the gifts our children received that year, I most anxiously anticipated seeing the look on my little boy's face when he spotted the red Jeep on Christmas morn.

He has never been a morning person, and he has never been real talkative, but I secretly believed the unveiling of the Jeep would transform him into the Roadrunner, or perhaps Bugs Bunny. He would get so excited that together, we would leap up and down and scream, "I love it!" And best of all, he would let me take a ride in it!

But things did not turn out that way. He just sat there on the rug in his Spiderman pajamas beside his pile of presents and stared into space, while I watched him carefully. Finally he spoke. "I like my bubbles," he said. There beside him, tucked underneath the wheel of the Jeep, sat a fifty-cent plastic bottle of bubbles.

As always, I remained calm and mature, even in my disappointment. "Yes, honey, the bubbles are nice. But did you see the Jeep? You know, that big red vehicle sitting in the middle of the house? It's yours! Do you like it? Do you? Do you?"

He looked at it and said, "It's nice."

In less than a few hours, he and every other small child in the neighborhood had taken a liking to the Jeep, and they were riding it all over creation while my husband plodded along behind them, making sure they were safe. Meanwhile, the plastic bubbles sat all alone on the front porch.

Somehow the phrase, "I like my bubbles" has stuck with me ever since that Christmas Day. Perhaps it serves as a reminder that it really is the little things in life that make us happy. Perhaps it is the fact that our children continually surprise us and that the only thing we can count on in any given situation is irony.

A toast: May we all be safe from severed limbs, and may we all "like our bubbles."

CPSIA information can be obtained at www.ICGtesting.com
Printed in the USA
LVOW08s2328020913

350645LV00001B/1/P